Potomac Fever

BOOKS BY FRED R. HARRIS

Potomac Fever
The New Populism
Now Is the Time
Alarms and Hopes

Potomac Fever

FRED R. HARRIS

W · W · NORTON & COMPANY · INC·

New York

Copyright © 1977 by Fred R. Harris
Published simultaneously in Canada
by George J. McLeod Limited, Toronto.
Printed in the United States of America.

First Edition

Library of Congress Cataloging in Publication Data

Harris, Fred R   1930–
  Potomac fever.

  Includes index.
    1. Harris, Fred R., 1930– 2. Legislators—
United States—Biography. 3. United States—Politics
and government—1945–   I. Title.
E840.8.H28A37 1977 328.73′092′4 ₍B₎ 76–30675

ISBN 0 393 05610 4

1 2 3 4 5 6 7 8 9 0

To the people of Oklahoma

Contents

Introduction

My wife, LaDonna, and I have always felt that people should, like snakes, shed their skins every now and then. We've been lucky enough to be able to do just that.

Our lives could be marked off in fairly distinct phases. There were the years when we were growing up in Cotton County, Oklahoma, as small-town, rural kids. There were the years when we were in Norman, Oklahoma, I as a student, and LaDonna working to help put me through school. There were the years when I was a young lawyer and a member of the Oklahoma State Senate, and LaDonna was involved with me in these activities, as well as in developing her own skills in the field of Native American rights and human rights generally.

Then, there were the twelve years we spent in Washington—from 1964 to 1976. During those years, Lyndon Johnson launched the War on Poverty and was brought down by the war in Vietnam, Robert Kennedy matured as a leader and deepened with the pain of his brother's death before himself becoming an assassin's victim, and Hubert Humphrey gave up his presidential ambitions at last and gained new national respectability and acceptance.

This book is about those years and those times. I've tried to write about them dispassionately and with good humor.

After our twelve years in Washington, LaDonna and I felt it was about time to move on to a new phase of our lives, in a new location. We'd camped and toured in New Mexico for more than twenty years, for we both have a great love of the area's archaeology and history. We'd long thought that some day we'd like to live there.

And so, one Saturday in July, following a delightful picnic with old friends and staff members, we boarded a sleek commercial jet in Washington, bound for Albuquerque.

As we rose into the sky on that hot summer afternoon, we were thrilled again by the sight, below us, of the great white dome of the nation's Capitol. We were leaving Washington with a good feeling about the country and its people, grateful for the chance we'd had to be a part of the nation's life in special ways.

It had been great being in Washington—and LaDonna and I had felt a certain sense of accomplishment during our years there. We had both matured and grown a great deal in that city.

Now, though, we wanted to trade the steamy banks of the Potomac River for the cottonwood shade of the Rio Grande. It was time for us to return to the region of the country where we'd both grown up. In New Mexico, we could be close to old friends back home in the state we'll always love, Oklahoma, without having to be bothered with old political divisions.

This book is not intended as a definitive history or autobiography. It is a fairly lighthearted, anecdotal memoir of twelve years in Washington. There are some lessons in it, true. But I hope there's enjoyment as well.

FRED R. HARRIS

Albuquerque, New Mexico
Fall, 1976

1

Not Exactly
a Social Disease

Potomac Fever is not exactly a social disease. It is a highly contagious affliction of the human mind. Many people have been known to catch it. I did on my first visit to Washington, D.C., and I probably still have a touch of it, although I think at last I have it under control.

All the experts agree that the symptoms of Potomac Fever are uniform and easily recognized: victims will do or say almost anything to return to, and stay near, the site where they were initially stricken—Washington, D.C.

In the earliest days of our nation, this site figured crucially in a purported three-way political deal which had the secondary effect of setting up the ideal conditions for Potomac Fever. Under the terms of the deal, the first three bills passed by the first Congress of the United States, meeting in New York City, established a private national-banking system, provided for a federal subsidy for construction of the Erie Canal, and permanently moved the capital of the United States down to where it would help Virginia.

At least that's the way the story was told by the late U.S. senator from Oklahoma Robert S. Kerr, perhaps the greatest bargainer the known world has ever produced. It was in the fall of 1962, and Senator Kerr and I were both speakers at a meeting of southeastern Oklahoma Democratic leaders, convened in the courtroom of the district court in McAlester, Oklahoma. The purpose of the meeting was to rally all Democrats, in a trumpet call for party unity, behind the Democratic nominee for governor of Oklahoma, W. P. Bill Atkinson, and the rest of the state party's nominees.

I myself had been an unsuccessful contestant for the gubernatorial nomination that year. Senator Kerr was the leader of the Oklahoma Democratic party, and he was hailed nationally as the "King of the Senate," that august body's most powerful member.

I'd first met Senator Kerr earlier that same year, when I was still a candidate for the Democratic nomination for governor. Rex Hawks, known in Oklahoma political circles as "Hawkeye," brought me the summons. Senator Kerr wanted to see me in his ninth-floor Oklahoma City office at the Kerr-McGee Oil Company, which he headed. Rex Hawks was Senator Kerr's political handyman, serving as his eyes and ears in the state. "The senator wants to look you over and get to know you better," Hawkeye told me.

I was thirty-one years old and had already served for nearly six years in the Oklahoma State Senate. I wanted to be governor. I knew state government well, and I had plenty of desire. I was full of ideas about what needed to be done in the state.

So, I presented myself to the uniformed policeman on the ground floor of the Kerr-McGee Building. The policeman didn't recognize me; very few Oklahomans did in those days. He called upstairs to make sure I had an appointment with the senator. I sat down on the black-leather couch and thumbed through a news magazine while he checked. Soon, a well-dressed and expensively coiffed secretary of medium age came smiling out of the elevator to greet me and take me up to the executive offices. Her manner was properly cheerful and carefully assured. I tried not to feel intimidated.

The elevator moved noiselessly to the top floor. The doors opened on a thick, brown carpet and an almost life-sized painting of Senator Kerr. We turned left, and then left again. Down the hall, past tasteful paintings and sculpture and fresh green plants that appeared to have been watered and sunned daily, the secretary led me to the walnut door of Senator Kerr's inner sanctum.

She paused briefly to knock and then opened the door. Senator Kerr, a man in his sixties, was up out of his chair, and he strode toward me in two or three huge steps, extending his massive hand. He was even taller than I had imagined from his pictures. His suit coat was off, revealing a blue-gray work shirt and black suspenders. An out-of-date, flowered red tie hung around his neck. His shirt collar looked too large, his baggy, gray trousers too loose at the waist. His face, with its high hairline and piercing eyes, was thinner than the jolly, roly-poly face the wirephotos showed. He'd recently lost a lot of weight. I learned later that he was in one of his intermittent weight-reducing periods, during which he regularly went down from around 240 pounds to around 215 pounds—thereafter, just as regularly, going back up again.

The huge office was modernistic, square and angular. Tall windows with tan draw drapes gave out on an imperial view of downtown Oklahoma City. The rich wood tones, leather furniture, dark-brown carpet, paintings—everything matched, and everything bore the unmistakable stamp of having been put together by a first-rate, expensive interior decorator.

Senator Kerr motioned me to a chair at one end of his huge desk, to his left, as he sat down again in the high-backed executive chair. Behind him were the flags of Oklahoma and the United States. On one wall was a large picture of Hyland Marchall, his prize Angus bull.

I'd read about Hyland Marshall and how Senator Kerr and his wizard veterinarian, Dr. Paul Kesee, had pulled off a real coup in buying the bull cheap. Hyland Marshall had had a venereal disease, but Dr. Kesee thought he could cure him—and after the purchase, he did. Hyland Marshall also had arthritis, a real problem for a herdsire. But Dr. Kesee overcame that difficulty too: Hyland Marshall became a herdsire, a very famous and expensive one, through the modern miracle of artificial insemination. No one knew what Hyland Marshall thought about this, but like everything else Senator Kerr had anything to do with, the purchase of this flawed bull turned out to be a huge financial success.

Senator Kerr's massive desk top was neat. There were no ash trays. A Bible lay flat on one corner of the desk, and there were several other books, upright. At the front was a little sign that read, ironically, "The buck stops here." A lot of bucks—the green kind —had, indeed, stopped there.

"What have you got on your mind, Fred?" he asked in his orator's voice, strong and measured and deep. A neat trick, I thought; *he* had summoned *me,* but I was suddenly made the supplicant. He took off his black-rimmed glasses in one grand sweep of his patrician hand and arm, leaned back in his chair, and fixed me with an unnerving gaze.

"I came to talk to you about my campaign for governor," I began, a little hesitantly. I leaned forward in my chair. My voice took on fiber, and I regained my confidence as I talked. I told him that I wanted to be governor because I wanted to change things. He listened intently. It seemed to me that he never even blinked his eyes. His expression never changed, and he said nothing. He didn't even nod his head, one way or another.

When I'd finished, he sat looking at me for long seconds. Abruptly, he sat back up in his chair, then leaned over on his desk, and said, "Fred, they *tell* me you're honest. You are the only one who *knows* for sure whether or not you are honest, but I am impressed by what they tell me about you."

He was silent again. It seemed like my turn once more. I told him I appreciated that comment.

"Are you sober?" he asked, his eyes seeming to search me as much as did the surprising question itself.

My first thought was, You don't suppose he means *right now?* But that whimsical notion passed quickly in the serious atmosphere. I knew that Senator Kerr was a militant teetotaler and a former president of the Oklahoma Baptist Convention. So I answered seriously.

"Yes, sir," I said. "I'll take a drink from time to time, but I have never found that to be either a personal or a political problem."

"That's what I like about you; at least you're honest," Senator Kerr said. "But let me ask you something. Did you know that I had the nerve to have the president of the United States in my home and not serve him liquor?" President Kennedy had recently visited Senator Kerr at his baronial estate at Poteau, in eastern Oklahoma, staying all night in the senator's ranch-style, limestone mansion.

"Yes, sir, I read that in the newspapers," I said.

"Can you think of any way that hurt me?"

"No, sir."

"Can you think of any way that helped me?"

"Yes, sir."

"Fred, do you know that there are people in this state who would continue to vote for me, even if I lost my mind, simply because I will not serve liquor in my home, even to the president of the United States?"

"I'm sure that's true, Senator," I said.

Senator Kerr leaned back in his chair again, looking straight at me all the time. Finally, he spoke once more. "Fred, you could make a lot of hay with some of these Baptist preachers if you were willing to say, 'I do not drink; neither does my wife. We do not serve liquor in our home, and we will not serve it in the governor's mansion.' "

"Senator," I said, "I won't *tell* you I'll do that, because I don't believe I *will* do it."

Senator Kerr said nothing for a time. Then, as abruptly as he had in asking the drinking question, he leaned forward once more and said, "Fred, are you humble?"

Somehow I sensed that this was a kind of riddle question. Kerr staffers later told me that it was a favorite of the senator's and that he judged people by their answers, saying, "If a man tells you he's humble, that's a sure sign he's not."

"I *think* I am, Senator," I said warily. "I have no trouble remembering where I came from." I had come from a small-town home, where making a living was a hard scrabble. My father had a third-

grade education, my mother an eighth-grade education. I was the
only member of my family ever to go to college. Senator Kerr,
now oil-rich, had been born in a log cabin. "I try to remember
where I came from," I said, "but I don't always show it—especially when I'm 'pitching' somebody like I'm 'pitching' you right
now."

I smiled. He didn't. But I got the impression that I had made
a passing grade.

He then asked me why I had opposed the turnpike bill in the
State Senate. I told him I had done so because the bill was the
result of a massive conspiracy against the interests of the people—
a conspiracy that involved some of the highest officials in the state
and a whole flock of big bankers, big engineers, and big lawyers.
Senator Kerr gave no hint, by word or by expression, of his own
opinion of the matter.

Then he stood up and extended his hand. The interview was
over. But he held on to my hand for some time and said, "Fred, if
I could do it without it hurting *you* or without it hurting *me,* I
would like to see you governor."

I was overjoyed. I thanked him heartily and left, all smiles. I
had gone down in the elevator and walked two blocks south, almost
skipping along as I passed Katz's drugstore, before I began to
analyze his last words. What had he said? "Fred, if I could do it
without it hurting *you* or without it hurting *me,* I would like to see
you governor."

This was an ingenious use of the English language. Kerr was
good at shaping words to his purposes. And he was also the best wit
Oklahoma had produced since Will Rogers. I had once heard him
employ both wit and language masterfully in a speech to an
Oklahoma City audience. On that occasion, he gave his version
of a press flap about reports that he'd said President Eisenhower
had no brains. Before a friendly and highly partisan crowd, Senator
Kerr first took note of the wave of critical comment which had
washed over him after he had uttered what many had taken to be a
crude and ungentlemanly slur on the highest official of the
government.

"In the first place," Senator Kerr then said, "I never charged that President Eisenhower had no brains. I said he had no *fiscal* brains."

Senators and representatives can "edit and correct" the *Congressional Record,* which supposedly reports, daily, every word spoken—and many which are not—by members of Congress in official sessions. Ordinary citizens often say to themselves, a day or week after an occasion which clearly called for an aphorism or some quotable repartee, "I wish I'd thought to say such and such." Senators and representatives *can* say it, retroactively, and there's the *Record* to prove they have done so.

News reporters had stated that Senator Kerr, following the floor speech in question, had later doctored the *Record,* altering, as time-honored tradition still permits, his otherwise reasoned attack on the government policies that had brought about tight money and high interest rates, and only then adding the word "fiscal" to his reference to Eisenhower. Kerr denied this before the Oklahoma City crowd.

But he did admit that he had spoken of the president's brains in a derogatory way. And he admitted, too, that he had been out of bounds in so doing.

His words were soaked with contrition, but as he spoke, there was the beginning of that well-known flicker of a smile around his otherwise riveting eyes. He swept off his glasses and paused for effect to let us know, deliberately, that we should get ready, because something funny was coming. We began to grin and nudge each other in anticipation.

"Our Republican brethren and their friends in the metropolitan press have undertaken to admonish me for having spoken critically, in any manner, concerning the brains of a man whom the people in their infinite wisdom have seen fit to elevate to the highest office it is within their power to bestow," Senator Kerr said. "And the Republicans are right, and I was wrong, as I now publicly confess."

Senator Kerr always spoke like that. And he always paused, almost interminably, for effect. He had the kind of assured stage presence and firm control of an audience that allowed him to indulge in galvanizing silences, frequently and at length, during any speech. At those times, he would pull off his glasses, straighten himself up to his full, awesome height, and gaze upon his hushed audience, almost menacingly, daring a wet baby to whimper or a consumptive to cough. He would play out the last measured moments of such an expectant silence, before finally delivering the stunning words that completed the thought and brought forth a bursting crescendo of laughter, or applause, or both. Now he did that before the Oklahoma City crowd.

"Yes, my Oklahoma friends, I was wrong and they were right," he boomed. "It is in the Christian way, which I learned in the Baptist church, that each of us should seek to profit through the admonitions of our fellows, and I have done so in this instance, as I freely admit.

"The Republicans have reminded me that, during all the long days of Franklin Roosevelt's presidency, they never, *never*—however vexed they felt themselves to be—uttered a single word in criticism of Franklin Roosevelt's crippled *legs*. Roosevelt, they rightly remind us, suffered from a physical affliction, not of his own making and not within his own power to correct. Those crippled legs were, they say, out of bounds to partisan comment—and they are right.

"I now see, my friends, by the same reasoning concerning what is, and what is not, a proper subject for political criticism, that I should never have made a comment of *any* kind concerning President Eisenhower's brains—because he cannot *help* it!"

Crescendo.

In the summer of 1954, fresh out of law school, I had worked actively in the unsuccessful campaign of former Governor Roy J. Turner against Kerr's re-election to the U.S. Senate. The senator was very much aware of that fact, but we nevertheless became friends in the last year of his life, campaigning together for the Democratic ticket in the fall of 1962, after I had lost the nomination for governor. We had several fairly intimate conversations during this period, and in one of those conversations, while we were flying into Lawton together for a campaign appearance, I asked him how he had become so powerful in the Senate. He answered me at once.

"First, I threw in right away with the Southerners in opposition to repealing the filibuster rule," he said. He went on to make clear that his motivation for so doing involved considerably more than just a personal desire for power: "Oklahomans vested me with one of their two Senate seats—one out of only ninety-six in that body when I came there—and I did not propose to start off by voting to diminish the power of that position to serve the interests of Oklahoma."

"Second," he continued, "I soon came to run three Senate committees at the same time. I became chairman of the Space Committee in my own right when Lyndon Johnson became vice-president. I ran the Public Works Committee because its actual chairman, Senator Dennis Chavez of New Mexico, was in the hospital most of the time.

"And I ran the Finance Committee because I was always prepared, because I studied my lesson, and because Senator Byrd was too old to run it."

There was something else, too, I knew. Senator Kerr was one of those people with a kind of instinct for power. He knew how to get power and how to use it.

He was a man of strong will—even in regard to things like ice cream. Following his speech and a later television appearance that time in Lawton, which was my home town, we started toward the airport in a black Cadillac driven by Lawton engineer Wyatt Hendrick. Realtor J. C. Kennedy, who later became state Democratic chairman on my recommendation, was also with us. As we headed toward the airport, Senator Kerr said very little. Slumped in the back seat, he seemed worn out and lost in his own thoughts.

All of a sudden, he became alert again. He sat up and spoke to me. "Is there a Dairy Queen on the way to the airport?" he asked.

"I believe there is one up on Second Street," I said. "It's not on the way to the airport, but we can swing by there easily."

"You're sure, now, it's a Dairy Queen—not one of those off-breed imitations?", he asked sternly.

I told him that I thought it was, indeed, a Dairy Queen, and Wyatt Hendrick turned north, off the highway and up Second

Street. But when we were still half a block away from the drive-in I'd remembered, Senator Kerr abruptly ordered, "Turn the car around!" It was a Dairy X stand. I had been wrong.

"Turn the car around, and let's go to the airport," Senator Kerr said, annoyed. "That's not a Dairy Queen; it's a Dairy X." I was later to learn that Lyndon Johnson had the same inordinate addiction to Dairy Queen ice cream. For him, too, no substitute was acceptable. Some said both Kerr and Johnson owned stock in the Dairy Queen corporation. In any event, it was a serious matter with both of them.

"I don't imagine that, blindfolded, you could tell the difference," I said to Senator Kerr, and laughed. He didn't laugh.

"If you would learn your town better, you'd be a more reliable guide for visitors," he said. Wyatt Hendrick swung the car around, and we sped toward the airport in silence.

At the Democratic meeting in the McAlester courtroom, I spoke first. I was one of the show pieces on that occasion: since I had myself lost the party nomination, it was especially appropriate that I call for party unity behind the nominee—toward the end that W. P. Bill Atkinson, rather than Republican Henry Bellmon, would become Oklahoma's next chief executive. I opened by saying, "I didn't come here to tell you that Bill Atkinson will be the best governor Oklahoma could *possibly* have had," and went on to state that he would certainly be better than Bellmon. I still think he would have been better, but he lost the election.

Senator Kerr was the concluding and featured speaker at the meeting. He left his chair at the counsel table in the courtroom and walked up to the low oak bar which separated him from the audience, his back to the judge's bench. He took out a blue handkerchief and wiped his face. The audience waited patiently in silence as he refolded the handkerchief and put it back in his hip pocket.

It was then that I first heard Senator Kerr's version of how the capital of the United States came to be on the Potomac River. In his speech, he called attention to news stories, then current, that the chairman of the Senate Finance Committee, Senator Harry F. Byrd, Sr., of Virginia, had decided against retiring from the Senate because he wished to keep Senator Kerr from becoming chairman of that powerful committee, under the inexorable rule of seniority which still governs such matters. It had been reported that this decision by Senator Byrd had been made at the urging of conservative financial interests that were against Senator Kerr because he was the most persuasive voice in the Senate against tight money and high interest rates, and was the nation's outstanding advocate of federal spending for dams and roads, especially if the dams and roads would benefit his own home state.

Senator Kerr confirmed this press speculation. And then he undertook to give his McAlester audience some background about the matter, in terms Oklahomans could understand.

"The Wall Street bankers threw a big dinner in New York to honor Harry Byrd, and all of the members of the Senate Finance Committee, myself included, were in attendance," Senator Kerr said. "The master of ceremonies, a New York banker, spent fifteen minutes introducing Harry Byrd as 'the greatest living watchdog of the federal treasury,' and Harry then got up and spoke for thirty minutes trying to prove it.

"Then, the master of ceremonies introduced *me* as the ranking majority member of the committee, and he made it clear in his brief remarks that I was *not* 'the greatest living watchdog of the federal treasury.'

"Well, I took it upon myself to give those New York bankers a lesson in American history," Senator Kerr said. Pause. Glasses off. Eyes crinkling a little at the edges. Here it comes, we thought.

"I told them that when the first Congress of the United States met in the then capital, New York City, Alexander Hamilton was anxious to pass a bill to set up a system of private banks, which would hold federal funds on deposit without paying interest and would loan out money to private citizens, charging interest. Hamilton made a deal for a part of the votes he needed by agreeing to support a *second* bill, to construct a canal for commercial freight from somewhere in New York to somewhere in Pennsylvania.

"But he still didn't have enough votes to pass his bank bill. So Hamilton went to Jefferson, and he said to Jefferson, 'If you'll support these other two bills, the bank bill and the canal bill, we'll agree to vote for and pass a *third* bill, to allow you to carve out a piece of Virginia and move the capital down there.'

"Jefferson wasn't certain about what he ought to do, so he went to talk to Washington. Washington told him, 'I'm not gonna be a party to any such deal, but if *you* are, you can't get a better one.' "

Pause. Expectant silence. When he sensed that we could hardly stand to wait for the punch line a second longer, Senator Kerr went on.

"So, I told those bankers, Jefferson agreed to the deal. Those three bills were the *first* three bills passed by the first Congress. Accordingly, a part of Maryland and a piece of Virginia were carved out and set up as the District of Columbia, the federal capital.

"Today, half the money the federal government spends every year is spent by the Pentagon alone, which is located across the Potomac River in Virginia, and I said 'Gentlemen, if I ever see the day when the federal government spends as much money in Oklahoma as it spends in Virginia, I will on that day become the greatest living watchdog of the federal treasury.' "

Thunderous applause.

Whatever the *exact* facts of history are, the capital *was* moved down to Washington, District of Columbia—on the banks of the Potomac River. And the first reported cases of Potomac Fever date almost precisely from the time of that move.

I contracted Potomac Fever just over 150 years later—in the summer of 1957. I was at that time twenty-six years old and newly elected to the Oklahoma State Senate. I came to Washington with Don Dage, the manager of the Cotton Electric Cooperative, which was located in Walters, the small, southwestern Oklahoma town where I'd grown up. I was the attorney for the Cooperative.

The trip to Washington with Don Dage marked only the second time I had flown on a commercial airline. The first had been earlier that same year, when I'd traveled to New York City with three other members of the Oklahoma state senate.

Two of the state senators had served in the Navy, and had been almost everywhere. The other two of us—Ben Easterly, who was an auctioneer, and I—had never been anywhere much. Our mission was to look into the question of how casualty insurance companies set their rates. But under the leadership of the more experienced members of our delegation, we also looked into the Latin Quarter, the Copacabana and a few other places, after our regular duties were finished.

On the New York City trip, we left Oklahoma City on an American Airlines four-motored, prop plane. We were hardly in the air before one of the ex-Navy men suggested that we move back to a table in the lounge and play poker. I'd never been a poker player, but I joined in, because I wanted to be a "good old boy." We played for small stakes—and I lost.

I lost for two reasons. First, I didn't know much about poker. Second, the plane was crashing, and I was the only one who was aware of it.

The game had just begun, when suddenly the motors, which had been laboring and groaning heavily, quit—or seemed to. I froze. But my companions took no notice, remaining attentive to their cards and the play.

Several times during that five-hour, nonstop flight to New York's LaGuardia, the motors seemed to me to go off and then on again. I never got used to it.

After dark, the situation was worse. Flames shot out of the rear of the motors, a clear indication that we were on fire. But the poker game continued. Nobody except me seemed aware that we were all about to die—and I was too embarrassed to mention it.

I'd stopped smoking about two weeks earlier, but long before we finally landed at LaGuardia, I was bumming cigarettes and chain-smoking them, one right after another.

The trip to Washington was better. By then, I knew what to expect, and I already felt myself an old hand at flying.

Don Dage was, and is, a wonderful friend to have, and he is at his best as a tourist guide. In 1957, he had already been to Washington more times than he could remember, but he knew I had never been there, and he took great delight in showing me around.

What a marvelous city! The first thing that impressed me about Washington was the foliage. During much of the year, western Oklahoma is dry. My dad always said that spring is the best time to *sell* a farm in Oklahoma. There's no other place as pretty at that time of the year. Summer, he said is the time to *buy* a farm. Then, western Oklahoma is dry and parched and the hot wind sears your throat going down—so the farm market's off.

But in full summer, Washington was green, lushly green, all trees and flowers. I'd never seen anything like it.

The history hit me next. It was here that Lincoln gave his Second Inaugural Address. And I reverentially read the words of that address carved into the high marble walls of the shrine where his massive statue sits. I saw the *actual* Declaration of Independence at the National Archives. I saw the changing of the guard at the Tomb of the Unknown Soldier.

Most important, I saw the Senate of the United States in session. The experience was both thrilling and disappointing. It was a thrill to see from the gallery senators like Stuart Symington of Missouri. I had studied them, almost unaware, as they appeared in the newspapers and on television. Now I recognized their faces, and I knew their home states.

The disappointment was that no more than three or four senators were ever on the floor simultaneously. One or two would from time to time wander in, and out again, while a solitary senator read a speech to the near-vacant chamber or, less frequently, engaged in a brief interchange with another member.

The presiding officer was clearly *not* Vice-President Nixon, or any recognizable senator. He was some unknown freshman member I could not identify.

In the Oklahoma Senate, presiding was an art and an honor, requiring a thorough knowledge of the rules. I was at that time already becoming adept at it.

In the Senate of the United States, however, presiding was regarded as drudgery, a kind of required pledge chore, and the individual performing it said or did whatever he was told to say or do by the Parliamentarian, stationed at a desk just below his own.

That was a disappointment, as was the empty chamber. While each lone member spoke in his turn and left, the presiding senator read his mail or leafed through a file of papers, taking no more notice of what was being said on the floor than if he had been a bored governess, looking up every now and then just to make sure that one of her charges hadn't set fire to something.

Could that presiding officer have been a Frank Church or a Jack Javits? Or perhaps he was a senator who lost his next re-election campaign and was never heard from again. Who knows now?

But after that first trip to Washington, I couldn't wait to get back. I wanted to show the city to my wife, LaDonna, and share it with her. I was fascinated, hooked.

The chance came quickly. In the spring of 1958, LaDonna and I were invited to chaperon five high-school and college students who had won a free trip to Washington, D.C., for submitting the best entries in a contest sponsored by the Oklahoma Democratic party. They had written essays and speeches on "Why I am a Democrat."

At the Oklahoma City airport, LaDonna and I met the young contest winners and their parents for the first time. I'm sure some of the parents were worried by our own youth. But we said our good-bys and assured them we would look after their children.

Our first problem in Washington was that there were seven of us in all, and District law prohibited so many people from riding in one cab. On each excursion, we had to search for *two* cabs, and were separated into two groups between points.

We thought we'd solved the problem once. At the Washington Monument, when we alighted from our two cabs, prepared to go to the top of that towering stela built in honor of the first president, the kids from the other cab rushed up to say that *their* driver was willing to wait and take all of us where we wanted to go next.

I quickly told them to hold him, to ask him to wait. A little later, tired and breathless, still excited about the great view of Washington we'd seen, we came out of the Washington Monument. Sure enough, there was our waiting cab.

The driver jumped out and held the door. "Senator," he said with an Italian accent, "I am honored to have you in my cab; the young people told me you were a senator."

I thanked him and told him we were very pleased to find a cabdriver who would take all seven of us. We crowded in.

"No problem, Senator," he said.

We drove up Constitution Avenue toward the Capitol. "What building is that?" I asked, motioning to our right.

"That's the National Art Gallery, Senator," he said, his voice carrying a slight tone of puzzlement.

"What's that building up ahead on the left?" I asked. "The one with the flag on it."

"Why, Senator," he said, now clearly puzzled, "that's your office building, Senator; that's where you senators have your offices."

Now, I knew what the trouble was. "No, you don't understand," I said. "I am a state senator, from Oklahoma."

He persisted. "That's what I mean," he said. "That's where all you state senators have your offices." But he sounded alarmed.

I patiently explained that there were senates in each of the states, just as there was a national senate. I said I was a member of one of those *state* senates.

He stopped the cab. "I can't take you any farther; I'll lose my license," he said. "I hope you understand."

We did. We paid him, got out, and went back to trying to flag *two* cabs. And we laughed a lot.

That day, we had lunch with the Oklahoma congressional delegation. Each member in turn introduced the young "Why I am a Democrat" winner from his district, and then the winner recited his or her speech or essay.

Most of these members of the House knew or had studied up on the individual from their district. Carl Albert, then House Democratic whip, knew all about his young constituent, Tony Basolo. In his introduction, Albert told of his long association with Tony's father in McAlester.

All of the others, too, were able to make very personal introductions, except for Representative Tom Steed. He'd never met his winner, and apparently no staff member had filled him in. So Steed had to improvise in his introduction of young Sam Hallman of Bristow.

Representative Steed talked a while, too long, about Bristow and Creek County and how he, Steed, had always had a hard time with the Republicans there. He finished by saying, "Sam Hallman is now going to speak on 'Why I am a Democrat,' and knowing the Republicans in Bristow and Creek County as I do, that is reason enough for Sam to be a Democrat."

Young Sam got up to polite applause. The small luncheon room that had been reserved for us in one of the House office buildings grew quiet. Sam cleared his throat nervously and began his memorized speech: "My parents are Republicans. . . ." The bursting laughter drowned him out. When he was finally allowed to continue, he went on to explain how he had personally decided on the Democratic party, despite his parents' affiliation.

Senator Kerr used to say, "Tom Steed is the only man I know who can corner you in the middle of a room." After the luncheon, it was hard to pry the embarrassed Steed loose from young Sam. "Some of my best friends in Creek County are Republicans," he kept saying to Sam, giving example after example of "good" Republicans he knew there.

We touched the toe of Will Rogers' statue in the Capitol for good luck. We went to Ford's Theatre. And we rented a car and drove down to George Washington's Mount Vernon estate.

I had already been to Mount Vernon, with Don Dage. Don and I, though, had gone there on a Wilson Line excursion boat, the best way. That's when I first contracted Potomac Fever.

Washington is a river city. What the Thames is to London or the Seine is to Paris—that's what the Potomac is to Washington. So Don Dage had brought me down by *river* to see Mount Vernon.

The trip was memorable, and coming back was the best part. The evening was growing dark as we passed under the Woodrow Wilson Bridge. Up ahead in the distance was the white, flood-lit Capitol dome, a sight that still thrills me.

Don and I were sitting in the bow, the cool evening breeze blowing against our faces. We had been silent for a long time, savoring the moment and the view.

"Fred," he said at last, "one day you'll be up here yourself."

Seven years later, I was.

2

Getting There
Is Half the Fun

Joe Willie Namath played in his first bowl game on New Year's Day, 1963. He was just a college sophomore at the time, but he had already quarterbacked Coach Paul "Bear" Bryant's Alabama Crimson Tide to a nine–one record in the 1962 regular season. His hair was shorter then, and his "Broadway Joe" image was further in the future than artificial turf.

But if bowl games were new for Joe Namath in 1963, they were old stuff for Charles Burnham "Bud" Wilkinson. He was America's winningest coach. His Oklahoma Sooners, standing eight–two for the season, were not the best team he'd ever coached, but still one more winning team from a football-mad state that had grown accustomed to nothing but winning. Bud Wilkinson's shy, dimpled smile, white hair, and becomingly modest manner were already well known to millions of American television viewers. And not just because of football. Hadn't sports-loving President Kennedy chosen him from among all other famous American sports figures to head up the new national physical-fitness program, to get Americans out of their armchairs and "moving again," literally as well as figuratively? It was a time of fifty-mile hikes, led by the president's own brother, Attorney General Robert F. Kennedy, a time when "Air Force exercises" were popular and new conditioning programs burgeoned in the public schools. Flab was out, and "get out and get with it" was in.

There was nothing flabby about Bud Wilkinson that New Year's Day as he trotted onto the field with his boys, a tall, lithe figure among Oklahoma's red-and-white uniforms, highlighted against an Orange Bowl field that was green enough to satisfy Hollywood's most picky technicolor experts.

Thousands of Oklahoma fans had come south to Miami's sun and fun. They recognized at once Wilkinson's white hair and familiar gray suit and lucky red tie, and the stadium could not contain their spontaneous roar of pride. For the Sooners, 1962 had not been the year of star players. Work horses like quarterback Monte Deere and fullback Jim Grisham were not flashy demigods; neither was a Darrell Royal or a Billy Vessels. Ralph Neely was playing on an alternate team, and Joe Don Looney's bizarre and troublesome personality had already dimmed the candle power of luminary status for him. Bud Wilkinson was the Oklahoma star, and the Sooner fans let him know they knew it.

Bud Wilkinson was a transplanted Oklahoman, but Oklahomans didn't mind. Their state was, after all, peopled with transplants, settlers who had come from every other state in the Union to stake out the newly opened Indian lands just before the turn of the century. Newcomers had always been able to make a place for themselves in Oklahoma, if they were of a mind to. Bud Wilkinson was of a mind to, and he had made a place for himself like no other.

A football star under Bernie Bierman in his native Minnesota, Wilkinson had learned the intricacies of the split-T formation from Don Faurot, the man who invented it. Wilkinson had been an assistant coach for Faurot's V-2 navy program football team during World War II, and he had learned well. Later, as an assistant to Jim Tatum at the University of Oklahoma, before succeeding to the job of head coach, Wilkinson had mastered the art of recruiting—of attracting not only players, but also backers. *True* magazine had written about Wilkinson's "One Hundred Millionaires." That was probably stretching it some, but he had cultivated enough construction-company executives and oil-company presidents to make sure that no boy who signed with him would lack a well-paying summer job. And if Wilkinson had cultivated Oklahoma's rich and powerful, he had also captivated the ordinary people of the state.

Oklahomans had needed a reason to cheer. They'd been down too long. The state had been laid out in 160-acre tracts, one to a family. But too much of the land was in the form of rocky, timbered hills or red-clay plains. The weather was capricious, too. And when the dry years of the 1930's had come, the hot, dust-laden winds had seared the feeble crops and blotted out the sun, leaving silt two inches deep on the floors of the frame houses. It was hard for those who left. John Steinbeck wrote of them in *The Grapes of Wrath.* It was hard for those who stayed, too. Hard to make a living, and hard to keep from getting mad when they were called "Okies."

And then, after the war, Bud Wilkinson's teams had begun to win. He became a rallying point. Oklahomans felt they had a reason for pride. Politicians began to court him and to try to edge into photographs with him. Rich people gave him cars. The president of the university announced that he wanted to build an institution "that the football team can be proud of."

Bud Wilkinson was good with the press, and he was good on television. The Kerr-McGee Oil Company sponsored his highly popular weekly television program, where, the day after each game, he moved little men around on a miniature football field and explained how it had all been done, his manner as winning as his teams. His players were in awe of him and were walking testimonials for him. He was the quintessential idol, and Senator Kerr and the late J. Howard Edmondson, then governor of Oklahoma, had been quietly importuning him to enter politics.

Attractive, young, redheaded Governor Edmondson was in the Orange Bowl stands that New Year's Day of 1963, when Oklahoma met Alabama in a clash of the titans, as the sports writers say. So was every other Oklahoman who could afford it. The rest of us were huddled around television sets back home.

It was a time when the president of the United States could still venture out among sports throngs, and the nation's number-one football fan, John F. Kennedy, was himself seated in a special box on the fifty-yard line that day.

Back in Oklahoma, in our basement den in Lawton, LaDonna and I had gathered with a few friends to watch the game on television. We hushed for the opening kickoff—and remained hushed, as it turned out, during most of the first half, because Oklahoma didn't do so well. Joe Namath had quarterbacked the Crimson Tide of Alabama to a 14–0 lead by half time. As our university's marching band came onto the field, the television announcer said that the Oklahoma fans in Miami seemed subdued and shocked.

We were soon to be shocked even more, for it was presently announced that Robert Samuel Kerr, the senior senator from Oklahoma, one of the two or three most powerful men in the United States and thus himself an object of great pride to Oklahomans, had just died in a Washington hospital of a heart attack, at the age of sixty-six. His death was a particular shock, both to those who knew him personally and to those who knew him only by his larger-than-life reputation, because somehow Bob Kerr had seemed the kind of person who would not ever die. He had apparently felt that way himself. His brother, Aubrey—"Uncle Aub," he was called—told me some months later that Senator Kerr had not signed a new will since the days before he'd become rich, and that his estate was in a mess. "Bob was always lecturing the rest of us about getting our business in order," Aubrey Kerr told me, "but he thought that he, himself, was too powerful to die."

At our house, and at countless other houses throughout Oklahoma, the Orange Bowl game was quickly forgotten. And just as well, too; Oklahoma never scored. Alabama won 17–0. Even on television a good deal of the half-time talk was about politics rather than football, about who would succeed Senator Kerr. The television cameras followed Oklahoma Governor Edmondson as he left his seat and went to confer with President Kennedy. It was pointed out that the governor would have to appoint someone to complete Senator Kerr's term in the U.S. Senate. Would he resign and have himself appointed? The television announcer mentioned that possibility. Others too were wondering about it.

J. Howard Edmondson was winding up four years as the youngest governor in Oklahoma's history, and by law he could not succeed himself. He had been elected in 1958 at the age of thirty-three, and in a few days would be turning over the job and honors to Oklahoma's first Republican governor, Henry Bellmon. Howard Edmondson was a meteoric Oklahoma figure. A crusading and photogenic Tulsa County prosecutor, he had attained the position of chief executive of the state through an unprecedented "prairie fire" television blitz.

When he started his campaign, I had already been a member of the Oklahoma State Senate for almost two years. At first, Edmondson was way back in a large field of much better known candidates. He was advocating all the right things, to my mind: repeal of prohibition, which was still the law then in Oklahoma; a merit system for state employees, then totally subject to the spoils system; central purchasing for all departments of the state government, which were then buying wastefully and sometimes on the basis of favoritism. But I didn't think he had a chance. He seemed too young and inexperienced, and he was too little known. In the last few weeks of the campaign, television changed all that.

I had used television extensively in getting elected to the State Senate, but nobody had ever conducted a *statewide* television campaign in Oklahoma. Howard Edmondson was the first, and his campaign was a novelty. Most Oklahomans had not yet heard of television cue cards or make-up.

Once, in the early days of that 1958 gubernatorial contest, one of the other candidates, Jim Rinehart, a State Senate colleague of mine and an old-timer in that body, came to Lawton. I paid a courtesy call on him at his hotel room following his scheduled speech. A number of his local supporters were having a beer with him, and Rinehart was entertaining them.

"Now, you take this redheaded kid, Edmondson," he said. "I keep hearing that the women like his looks on television. But I'm going to tell you something that you're not going to believe. That kid *reads* every word that he says on television from big cards that somebody holds up in front of him." There were murmurs of disbelief.

"It's the truth," Rinehart continued. "And I'll tell you something else that's worse. They put *make-up* on him before he goes on TV." General shock!

"They sure do. A boy that works at WKY told me himself."

It was a choice morsel of gossip, repeated many times by Rinehart's supporters, but to no avail. Nothing, it turned out, could offset Edmondson's superb voice and dynamic television manner, selling the kind of government reform Oklahomans were hungry for.

I made speeches for Edmondson and introduced him when he came to my area. And after he had been swept into office, he asked for my advice. Humility doesn't come easy to a thirty-three-year-old governor, elected by a landslide, and I cautioned him about that. I told him that if he was smart enough to be elected governor, he was smart enough to figure out how to *be* governor.

But Edmondson got off to a bad start. He first announced that he wouldn't live in the old governor's mansion until it had been totally redecorated. He spent a lot of money refurbishing and modernizing his office in the capitol building. And he refused to court the old mossbacks in the Senate, many of whom, like my friend, Senator Don Baldwin of Anadarko, an honest and powerful man, started out willing to help the governor with much of his program.

Worse, Edmondson soon let himself become the darling of the country-club set and the contractors. His friends profited from the building of a turnpike, and he and I got crosswise on that. He picked up an image as a playboy, and was portrayed in this light in *Time* magazine. He'd gained enough enemies by pushing good reforms and programs. He didn't need any more.

After it was too late, he decided to try to build some bridges back to the legislature. But even this was mishandled. He sent one of his least attractive and most flamboyant aides, an individual widely suspected of being a bag man, to see Senator Baldwin.

"The governor wanted me to come and ask your advice about what he should do to establish better relations with the Senate," the aide told Baldwin.

"Well, he must not be *too* worried," Baldwin said. "I'm fairly available, and I'd be quite willing to talk to him in person."

The aide explained that the governor was very busy, but promised to repeat word for word to the governor any advice which Senator Baldwin cared to give.

"That boy must do like it says in the Bible," Baldwin said, at last.

"Sir?" the aide questioned, puzzled.

"He must be born again."

By New Year's Day, 1963, Edmondson and I had become totally estranged. We'd had harsh words in private, and we had disagreed strongly in public. Our most bitter fight had been over the building of that new turnpike. In an hour-long, carefully detailed speech on the floor of the Oklahoma State Senate, the only such speech ever printed in full in the *Senate Journal,* I had accused the governor's friends of attempting to profit unconscionably from the sale of the toll-road bonds and the letting of the construction bids. I had gone to the governor's mansion alone one night and subtly threatened him with a grand-jury investigation if he persisted in his support of their schemes. And I had won in that instance, rewriting the legislation so as to better safeguard the public interest. We were no longer friends.

J. C. Kennedy, who was my neighbor in Lawton, and who had been appointed to the State Highway Commission, called me immediately following the television announcement of Senator Kerr's death. "Ned Shepler and I are going to send the governor a telegram in support of his own appointment to the Senate," he said. "What do you think?"

I said I didn't think much of it. I didn't think the people would like the idea of the governor resigning nine days before his term expired and having his friend, Lieutenant Governor George Nigh, who would then become governor, appoint him to replace Kerr. I said I didn't think he would subsequently be able to gain election in his own right.

"Who then?" Kennedy asked. I suggested the possibility that Howard Edmondson might appoint his brother, Ed Edmondson, then a member of the House of Representatives, to fill the vacancy. "He'd make a better senator, and he might be able to win the next election on his own," I said. I also mentioned that one of Senator Kerr's sons would probably be interested in the appointment.

Senator Baldwin also called me. "They're already fighting over Uncle Bob's garments before they lay him in his coffin," he said. It was true.

I felt sadness at Senator Kerr's death. He was a big man, and a complex one. There was both good and bad in him, as in us all. I felt a political loss, too. I intended to be a candidate for governor again in 1966, and I had had reason to expect Senator Kerr's support. I knew that although we had only lately become acquainted, he had spoken very highly of me to members of his family and to his closest friends.

Edmondson resigned and had himself appointed to the Senate. In so doing, he earned the undying enmity of the Kerr family— Grace Kerr, the senator's widow, and his three sons and a daughter. They felt they had been dealt with cavalierly. The senator's eldest son, Robert S. Kerr, Jr., announced that he would run against Edmondson in 1964, when an election would decide who would hold the office during the final two years of Kerr's term.

A former governor, Raymond Gary, let it be known that he too would run against Edmondson. I had served in the State Senate during the last two years of Governor Gary's tenure. I liked him personally, and I admired his courage in implementing the 1954 U.S. Supreme Court decision on school integration. But we had disagreed on a number of other issues. He was more rural in outlook, I more urban. He was more a part of the old order, I a member of the "good-government crowd."

Raymond Gary was a country schoolteacher by trade. He had been elected a county superintendent of schools in his home county in southern Oklahoma, then state senator, and finally, governor.

Gary liked me because after I had lost out in the 1962 Democratic gubernatorial primary, in which he was also a candidate (for a second, non-consecutive term), I had refused to endorse his run-off opponent, and had remained neutral during the run-off primary (which he had lost).

My best friend in the Senate during the time Gary was governor was a tall, forty-year-old, country-smart all-round good old boy from Durant—Keith Cartwright, now dead. Keith was the seventh son of a seventh son. "I'm supposed to be able to cure all sorts of things, like warts and ringworms," he would say. Keith had grown up in Wapanucka, a town of about five hundred people in southeastern Oklahoma. He told a lot of stories, and they all had a Wapanucka setting. "We'd go into town every Saturday," he told me one time, "and Mama would warn all us kids to stay out of the main street because, sure as the world, they'd be a runaway before the day was over. Runaway teams of horses was our second most exciting thing in Wapanucka. The *most* exciting thing was a dogfight. More'n likely the owners of the dogs would themselves get in a fight before it was over.

"Well, one time a traveling tent show came to Wapanucka to put on a play. They set up in a vacant lot, which wasn't hard to find. The word spread fast, and the tickets went like hot cakes.

"But the leading lady got sick, and the manager of the show said, 'She ain't got much of a part in this play, so just go out on the street and hire me anybody you can find for five dollars, and I can teach her what to do.' So they did; they went out onto the street and hired a woman, and the manager taught her what she was supposed to do. All she had to do was at one place in the play, when the leading man shoots her with a blank pistol, she had to break a little capsule of ketchup on her breast and fall down dead.

"Well, the night of the play came, and every soul from twenty miles around was there. We drove in in a wagon. It was a hot night, and the tent was packed and people standing up all around the sides.

"Pretty soon, it comes the part where the leading man shoots the leading lady with the blank pistol, and the woman does it just right. She breaks the capsule of ketchup on her breast and falls down dead. The leading man, he walks up to the front of the stage and says in a dramatic voice, 'My God, my God, what have I done?'

"Just then, there's an old boy in the back of the tent that's caught up in the action, and he hollers out in a loud voice, 'I'll tell you what you've done, you sumbitch; you've just shot the only whore in Wapanucka!' "

Keith had only a high-school education, but he was smart enough to know right from wrong. During each session of the State Senate, he deliberately chose to handle the hottest question. Ten years before prohibition was finally repealed in Oklahoma, he was repeal's most ardent advocate. And he was thrown out of the Baptist church in Durant for that effort. When Raymond Gary was governor, Keith and I teamed up to oppose him on a matter close to Gary's heart.

The governor was pushing hard for a bill, backed by the Oklahoma Gas and Electric Company and the Oklahoma City Chamber of Commerce, to authorize the use of state and federal highway funds to pay the utility company for removing its lines from the public highway right-of-way, so that the highway could be broadened. At this time, the company could not *legally* demand payment for such removal.

Keith and Gary were good friends, and Keith went down to the governor's office to try to talk him out of his support for the measure. Gary listened politely while Keith explained to him how it was simply wrong to use public money to pay a company to do something the law required it to do anyway. But the governor wouldn't budge, and, as Keith liked to tell it, Gary finally, in confidential tones, explained one reason why.

"Keith," he said, "they've promised to name that new highway after me, if I can get this done."

Keith had a counterargument. "Listen, Governor," he said, "there's nothing permanent about 'em naming anything after you. You remember they named that turnpike after Johnston Murray while he was governor, and as soon as he went out, they renamed it, for Will Rogers. If I was ever to have something named after me, like a bridge, say, or even a culvert, I'd want my name worked into the structure in such a way that if they ever took my name off of it, the damn thing would fall down."

But Raymond Gary was not persuaded. He beat Keith and me. The bill was passed. The new highway was built, and was christened the "Raymond Gary Expressway." And as soon as the governor went out of office, it was renamed the "Eastern Bypass."

Later, when Howard Edmondson was governor, Keith and I led another, more bitter fight, which placed us in stronger opposition to Raymond Gary, who, although out of office, was still, as a former governor, the leader of the rural forces in Oklahoma and the old guard. Keith and I went to North Carolina to study the highway system there, because some years before, the jurisdiction over building and reparing rural roads in that state had been taken away from the powerful county commissioners and centralized in the state highway department. Keith had at one time sold supplies to county commissioners in Oklahoma, and he could give chapter and verse to show how blatantly crooked some of them were. We liked what we saw and heard in North Carolina, and when we came back to Oklahoma, we attacked the county commissioners and introduced a bill to take away their road-building powers.

It turned out that repealing prohibition was a cinch, despite the combined opposition of a lot of preachers and bootleggers, compared to taking on the county commissioners. There were three of them in each of Oklahoma's seventy-seven counties, and every one had done some favor for nearly every voter in his district. Howard Edmondson supported us, and Raymond Gary and the rural forces opposed us. We lost. But Keith and I and our two other Senate cosponsors—we were called the "Four Horsemen"— were able to get through some important reforms before the fight was over. I was the only one of the Four Horsemen who survived the next State Senate election. "No use crying over Keith," Senator Baldwin told me. "He done his damndest and he liked it, and when your ass is greased, you're bound to slide."

Talk of the U.S. Senate race dominated the capitol corridors and the hotel rooms in Oklahoma City when the state legislature convened in early January, 1963. The roster of serious candidates seemed to be well set. Coach Bud Wilkinson, it was understood, had finally given in to the pressure on him to enter politics—Republican politics, as it developed. He had come to a private decision—later to be made public—to quit coaching, resign as chief of President Kennedy's physical-fitness program, shift his registration from the Democratic to the Republican party, and change his name legally to Charles B. Bud Wilkinson, so that the voters would know, when they saw his name on the ballot, that he was, indeed, the legendary "Bud" who had made so many people proud to be Oklahomans.

J. Howard Edmondson, having been appointed, was the sitting senator, and he was, of course, already running for re-election. He was spending almost as much time in Oklahoma as he was in Washington. The papers were filled with reports of his new Senate activities, and the mails were clogged with his newsletters to the voters. The so-called "Kerr people," who formed a close-knit and politically powerful network throughout the state, bitterly opposed Edmondson. They were harshly critical of his having had himself appointed to Senator Kerr's seat without, they felt, the proper deference to the wishes of the Kerr family.

The old-guard, rural, and antireform forces also bitterly opposed Edmondson, as did the "drys," those who had been against the repeal of prohibition. The candidate of this large, amalgamated group was the former governor of Oklahoma and former president of the Oklahoma Baptist Convention, Raymond Gary. And he was gearing up, renewing contact with his loyal supporters in each of the state's counties. It was generally recognized that Howard Edmondson had virtually no support in the rural areas and that Raymond Gary was weak in the cities.

Somewhere in between was Robert S. Kerr, Jr. Young Kerr was as tall as his father and looked a great deal like him. He was the beneficiary of the almost automatic support of the Kerr people. But it was already being said that he was no Bob Kerr. For one thing, he was not a speaker, and his painfully halting platform appearances were inevitably being compared unfavorably with the masterful performances of his late father. For another thing, young Kerr was shy and did not relish shaking hands with hordes of people and asking for their votes. He'd never liked politics, which he'd regarded as his father's business, not his. And this attitude showed.

People soon began to say that young Kerr would never actually file as a candidate for the Senate, that he'd only been pushed into political activity by his mother and the rest of the family. Even one of his uncles, a brother of the late senator, said to me privately, "The boy will never go." And he set me thinking with an additional, pointed statement: "You better hold yourself ready, Fred; the people may have to send in a substitute."

This was an intriguing thought to me, but not a very serious one at the time, although a number of other people had spoken to me along the same lines. I was certain that Robert S. Kerr, Jr., *would* run for the Senate. More important, my mind was still on running for governor again. And I was much more prepared to be governor than I was to be senator, I thought.

Senator Baldwin had told me I was crazy when I had tried running for governor the first time. A seat in the U.S. Senate was what I ought to be looking for, he had said. Baldwin, who gave nicknames to everyone, including Oklahoma's two U.S. senators, Kerr and A. S. "Mike" Monroney, called me "Freddie" or "the Babe," since I was the youngest, or "baby," of the Senate members. "Be patient, Freddie," he had said. "One of these days Uncle Bob and old Macarony will pass out of the picture, and then it will be your turn. Suppose you did run for governor and got elected; you'd make a good one, maybe the best we've ever had, but then you'd wind up going out of office as a has-been at thirty-four, not able to get elected to anything else."

It was true that the office of chief executive had been a graveyard for most of the Oklahoma politicians who had held it. But I had told Senator Baldwin back then, with youthful confidence, that this was not an immutable rule. I might like to be a senator eventually, I had admitted, but I felt that I ought to work up to it. I had said, too, that a person like me, with no big name and no money, could never be elected to the senate without first having served as governor.

In the early spring of 1963, Senator Baldwin was one of those who was telling me to give some thought to the possibility that I might have to run for the Senate. "Young Bob's liable to pull up lame in the backstretch, Freddie, and they may put the saddle on *you,*" he said. He proved to be right.

What makes a person run for the U.S. Senate? A desire to serve others? Vanity? It's some of both with most individuals, and I'm sure it was with me, although I hope I'm right in thinking that the former had more to do with my decision than the latter. People said to me that Washington was the place where one could do the most good, because the real power was there. In each of us is something that wants to leave a mark, that wants immortality at least in remembrance after we're gone. A few years back, a country song title put it pretty well: "I Don't Want to Be Just a Line in the *Oklahoma City Times.*" High public office affords that kind of opportunity—an opportunity to perform good service that will be remembered and to satisfy one's vanity. How the mix comes out is the big question.

There are great personal rewards and great personal risks in standing for public office. For all of us, those who run for office and those who don't, the self-image is the result of a mirroring process. We *do* see ourselves as others see us, or at least as we think they see us. Each of us is constantly revising his self-image on the basis of his perception of how other human beings react and respond to him. Am I a good person? John seems to think so; he likes me. Am I a mess? Mary seems to think so; she's disappointed in what I said. The process is a continuing one, going on hour by hour and day by day. Some of us worry about it too much; some of us, too little. For most people, the process is altogether *informal,* but for politicians, there is the formality of regular elections. Success at the polls is a kind of certified stamp of approval from one's fellows. Loss of an election is a kind of stamp of disapproval, equally certified. There's no guessing about it.

Young Bob Kerr, it turned out in the spring of 1963, did not want to be in the U.S. Senate badly enough to risk a possible rejection by the voters. He pulled out of the contest. Although I had already suffered defeat in the last gubernatorial race and knew that it would be painful for me, personally and politically, to put two losses back to back, I decided to seek the nomination. My desire to be a U.S. senator was greater than my fear of the possibility of another defeat.

And I had a lot to go on. I had been a conscientious state senator. I had made a creditable campaign for governor. And I inherited a good deal of the backing of the Kerr people, who could support neither Edmondson nor Gary in the Democratic primary. There had been some business dispute between Senator Kerr and Raymond Gary that had left both personal and political scars.

Getting elected to public office requires skill in communication and persuasion. It requires the espousal of at least seemingly sensible positions on issues. And it involves a great deal of luck. I was able to become a candidate for the U.S. Senate in 1963 only because a vacancy had been created when Senator Kerr died. I was able to be elected because no perfect candidate ran and because there was sizable opposition to all the other candidates.

Running for office is a peculiar business. The outcome probably depends a great deal more on the candidate's personality—or, more accurately, on the perception by the public of that personality and character—than on the issues. Stands on issues, or the absence of stands, help to reveal what sort of *persons* candidates are—where their hearts are, how they think, how they make up their minds, and whether they can stand the heat. The personality and character of a man or woman in office will still remain after the transitory issues of a campaign have faded.

The most salable personal asset of a candidate is what we used to call in Oklahoma, in prefeminist days, being a "good old boy." Is he one of us? Does she know how we live and what we think and want? These are the basic questions the voters ask—and rightly, in a democracy. And it's because they ask these questions that personal appearances and endless handshaking are so important. People draw their conclusion about a candidate mostly from personal contact with the candidate or from the comments of those—friends or observers and reporters—who have had this personal contact. Advertising serves to reinforce opinions which have been formed in that way; it doesn't change many minds. By filing time—February, 1964—I had already been to *every* single town in Oklahoma, including some consisting of no more than a store and a post office, and I had put together a list, indexed by name and town, of every person I had met personally who had told me he or she would support me for the U.S. Senate.

This kind of face-to-face campaigning is highly effective. Voters get a chance to see and talk with and size up the candidate personally. Those who are convinced become missionaries; they spread the gospel to others. This kind of campaigning can also produce some funny, and sometimes embarrassing, incidents. I've had my share.

When I first ran for the State Senate, twenty-five years old and not too long out of law school, I was not very well known in one very important part of my district. And a candidate needs a conversation opener; most people are as resistant to campaigning politicians as they are to cold-canvassing insurance salesmen. I was unknown then in the town of Elgin, but my sister Sue had married J. T. Stauffer, a young man who had grown up there. So when I was campaigning in Elgin, I would say, "I'm Fred Harris, running for the State Senate. You might know my sister Sue; she married John Stauffer's boy J. T." People would invariably say, "Oh, you're J. T's brother-in-law," or, "Sure, I've known old John Stauffer for thirty years." And then I could get a conversation going.

The trouble with this kind of routine is that if one is not careful, it comes to be a kind of rote exercise. That's what happened to me. I didn't really know John Stauffer, but I was, in a way, trading on his name in Elgin, and I got caught at it. One Saturday afternoon, I went into Homer Hise's Hardware Store there and began shaking hands with about a dozen men who were standing around. An older man sat off to the side, watching the process. "I'm Fred Harris, running for the State Senate. You might know my sister Sue; she married John Stauffer's boy J. T.," I said several times, working through the group.

Finally, I came to the older man. I shook hands with him too, and gave him one of my cards. "I'm Fred Harris, running for the State Senate," I said, but before I could go on with the rest of my routine, he interrupted.

"Yes," he said, "I'm John Stauffer."

Only the raucous laughter of the onlookers kept me from making matters worse by completing the too-automatic spiel: "You might know my sister Sue; she married your boy J. T."

An essential part of any successful political campaign is convincing those who are already committed to the candidate that they have great influence, greater than they realize. Some of this convincing can be done person-to-person. "You are an opinion molder," we would tell our supporters over and over in countless meetings and coffees during the U.S. Senate campaign. "Most people do not have an opinion in this campaign yet, or if they do, they are too unsure of themselves to express it. They are afraid their candidate can't win, and they don't want to appear ridiculous. You *do* have an opinion, and if you're not afraid to express it—if you're not afraid to say, 'I know Fred Harris; he's the best man in this race; and he's going to win'—you'll make that prediction come to pass."

Effective political advertising must be aimed at reinforcing the already favorable opinions of supporters, giving them ammunition, and causing them to be more outspoken in the candidate's cause than they might otherwise be. Early in the campaign for the U.S. Senate, I secured the services of a brilliant and hungry young advertising man named Ross Cummings. Years before, when we were both students at the University of Oklahoma and he was editor of the *Wagon Wheel,* a campus humor magazine, he had caused the Regents-enforced demise of that publication by devoting what turned out to be its last issue to a photographed chronicling of a scantily clad visit to the campus, which he had engineered, by Lily Christine, the Cat Girl, a well-known stripper of the time. Ross was not a man of conventional thinking. He had ideas, several a day, some good and some bad.

A good candidate can reject bad ideas. What he can't survive is having *no* ideas. I was proud of having been a Phi Beta Kappa student, in political science, and having been graduated from law school at the head of my class. Ross talked me out of going whole hog on publicizing assets of this sort. "People for whom that is important will find it out, anyway, Fred," he said. "Besides, if I was running for the Senate, and someone called me a Phi Beta Kappa, I'd bust 'em in the mouth; down in Idabel they think that's a drinking fraternity."

Ross had the idea that there was no inherent reason why paid political advertisements should not arouse almost as much interest as political news. People did get stirred up about campaigns, he said, but unfortunately, the excitement came largely from newspaper stories and broadcast news over which the candidate had very little control. We decided to put most of our advertising money into one-minute television commercials, and these were to be different from the usual—they would be made on location. If I was going to say something about how hard most Oklahomans were finding it to make a living, we would film the statement at a factory gate or in a main-street café or barbershop. If I was going to advocate the development of Oklahoma's waterways, I would stand on a riverbank to say my piece for the cameras.

The first such commercial we produced was about cattle prices. We took a crew down to my dad's small farm in southwestern Oklahoma to film the commercial. I was to stand in front of a cattle lot while my dad, my uncle Jack, and some neighbors kept the cattle bunched up behind me. The day was overcast. Special lights had to be set up. Fat black extension cords made the barnyard look like a den of snakes. Special aluminum reflectors were set up to focus what sunrays were able to break through the clouds. The onlookers were fascinated. The place was like a Hollywood set.

"Okay, herd the cattle back there. Okay, lights. Quiet, everybody, for sound. Okay, camera. Fred, on cue."

And on the signal, I would begin my memorized forty-five-second statement on cattle prices: "Farming is the backbone of Oklahoma's economy. . . ."

"Cut! There's something wrong with the sound." The rest of us would have to stand around while the technicians got the trouble ironed out. Then, again, cattle bunched up, lights, quiet, camera, and my statement.

"Farming is the backbone of Oklahoma's economy. . . ."

"Cut! I'm sorry, there was somebody back there in the picture with the cattle." And it was all to do over again.

And again, and again, and again. Over and over, I said, "Farming is the backbone of Oklahoma's economy. . . ." It took three hours to film a forty-five-second statement. During one of the technical interruptions, as I stood, bored, waiting to start again, my uncle Jack came over to me. "Bud," he asked, "if you just *had* to say, what would you say is the backbone of Oklahoma's economy?"

Because of television, I soon became a celebrity. People recognized me and stopped me on the street. I was asked for my autograph. By the time of the Democratic primary, in May, 1964, I was as well known as Raymond Gary and Howard Edmondson. I ran a close second, nosing out Gary in that contest. Edmondson, though the top candidate, received far from a majority vote, so there was a runoff three weeks later, between the two of us. The Gary forces joined with mine, once their candidate had been eliminated, and I beat Edmondson in every county but one in the runoff.

The pivotal event in the campaign against Edmondson was a televised debate between us, shown throughout the state. Edmondson had wanted the debate because he was a consummate debater. I had wanted it because I believed the "Nixon-Kennedy effect" would work to my advantage. Edmondson was older and better known, and he enjoyed a deserved reputation as an excellent speaker, very much at home on television. I felt that if I could just hold my own, just come off with a draw or a near-draw, the televised debate would be helpful to my campaign. And that's the way it turned out. After the debate, even though I certainly had not bested Edmondson, I no longer seemed too young and inexperienced to most voters—their view of me had changed, much as their view of Kennedy had changed after his debates with Nixon.

It was a long time between May, when I was nominated for the Senate, and November, when I was to go up against Bud Wilkinson, who had won the Republican nomination without a contest. Gaining his party's nomination without an opponent turned out to be a disadvantage to Wilkinson; he was deprived of the opportunity to generate early excitement and interest in his candidacy. Back at filing time, several of my friends had asked me, "How can you ever hope to be as well known as Wilkinson?" My answer had been that if I could beat two former governors in the Democratic primaries, while Wilkinson was coasting along, by the time of the general election I would be as well known as he, and all the excitement and momentum would have developed in my campaign, not his. That was about the way it worked out.

After the nomination process was completed, and before the general-election campaign heated up, there was a kind of lull in voter interest in the Senate race. It was a good time to take stock and make plans. As our slogan against Wilkinson we adopted "Prepared for the Job," emphasizing his inexperience in politics and government, in contrast to my experience. Wilkinson was actually a right-winger, almost a Bircher, and a strong supporter of Goldwater for president, but his statements had been characterized by generalities and platitudes, and we worried over how to smoke him out. We worried, too, about how to cut his highly popular and almost sacrosanct image down to size without causing a backlash of voter resentment. Was there a way to get people to laugh a little about Wilkinson's candidacy?

During the lull after the primary, I went off to Atlantic City as a delegate to my first Democratic National Convention. It was an occasion of hoopla and excitement. Lyndon Johnson, who had succeeded to the presidency upon John Kennedy's assassination, was renominated in what seemed an extravaganza of blaring bands, wild demonstrations, and mass choruses of "Hello, Lyndon." Liberal war horse Hubert Humphrey became his running mate, after the president had toyed for a while with my own choice, Senator Eugene McCarthy, Humphrey's colleague from Minnesota.

I was given a place on the program, reading a part of the platform, at the 1964 convention. The idea was to provide some television exposure for the party's nominees for contested Senate seats. And what a demonstration my friends put on when I was introduced in the monstrous hall! It was almost as big a demonstration as Humphrey's. But, alas, it was to be of no help back home. The cameras had cut away from the platform reading, and the television audience was being presented instead with commentary and interviews about credentials challenges and other —to my mind—less important subjects, such as who Johnson's choice for vice-president would be. Nevertheless, it was an exhilarating experience.

During the lull before the general election, I also went to Washington, as my party's nominee for the Senate. I attended a briefing for congressional candidates, took a publicity picture with President Johnson, and talked with the head of the Senate Democratic Campaign Committee, Senator Warren Magnuson of Washington, who promised a financial contribution to my campaign. "We gave money to Howard Edmondson's campaign in the primaries, because he was the incumbent, but now, you're our nominee and we'll help you," he said.

While I was in Washington, Lawrence Spivak, the venerable moderator of the long-running NBC "Meet the Press" program, sent word that he wanted to speak to me, and I went to see him at the sprawling Sheraton Park Hotel. Spivak, a small, self-assured man, at once stern and cheerful, ushered me into his cluttered office, the walls of which were covered with autographed pictures of the famous people who had appeared on his show over the years. I was pleased to meet him, and I wanted to make a good impression. But after campaigning for months, shaking hands with thousands, I had a grip as strong as a champion arm wrestler's. I grasped Spivak's outstretched hand, and squeezed. He yelped with pain and almost went down to his knees before I let go. Unbeknownst to me, several fingers of Spivak's right hand were inflamed, and undue pressure on them was highly unpleasant for him. Not too good a start, I thought, and apologized.

I then sat down across from Spivak's desk and lit a cigarette. He asked me to put it out, calling my attention to a sign on his desk which I had not noticed until then: "Please—No Smoking." "I am allergic to those things," he said. So much for the good impression.

We got down to business. He said he wanted to have Wilkinson and me appear together on "Meet the Press," and he gave me several alternative Sundays from which to choose. I told him I would let him know after I got back to Oklahoma and could check my schedule. I was stalling, because I didn't want to do it. He said that Wilkinson had agreed. I promised to get back to him right away, and then we spent ten or fifteen minutes in a warm chat centering on Senator Kerr, who, Spivak observed, had been about the best guest he had ever had on his program. "This is a program where you can do yourself a lot of harm or a lot of good; it's up to the guest," he said. "If you lie or evade, it shows; if you tell the truth or admit you don't know the answer, you come across." He said that Senator Kerr, whether you liked his positions or not, had given the impression of being straightforward, of saying what he thought, and that he had been as tough as his questioners. Spivak remembered one program, at the time the senator was seeking the Democratic nomination for president, during which Kerr was asked the inevitable question: "Would you accept the vice-presidential nomination?" Senator Kerr, Spivak said, had fixed the questioner with his most intimidating stare and had responded, "Do *you* have it to offer?"

I was later to become friends with Lawrence Spivak and to appear on "Meet the Press" a number of times. But in the campaign in Oklahoma in 1964 we had made an early decision that I would not debate or appear jointly with Wilkinson, for fear of what might be called the "Salinger-Murphy effect." Pierre Salinger, who had been President Kennedy's press secretary, and George Murphy, the former film actor, were running against each other in 1964 for the office of U.S. senator from California, and they engaged in a televised debate, upon Salinger's challenge. In the debate, Salinger, the more experienced of the two in politics and government, came across as a martinet. Murphy, who was not expected to excel in such a forum, came across as a likable, nice guy. And Murphy won the election. We were afraid a debate with Wilkinson might have that kind of effect, and we didn't think I had to debate to win. We were wrong in this decision for several reasons, and later changed our minds. But by then, it was too late for a joint appearance on "Meet the Press."

As the nominee for the Senate, I found raising money much easier than before; hitherto, this had been the worst problem of the campaign. I had started out with no money and no firm promises of financial support. The first funds came from a $3,000 personal loan I obtained at the Security Bank and Trust Company in Lawton. We raised another $16,000 from three dinners, at which the price was twenty-five dollars a couple, payable at the rate of five dollars a month.

In all my life, I never was in a campaign which most of the observers and the "smart money" thought I could win. And I never had the money when I started. In a situation like mine, raising money is not a task separate from campaigning; it is part of the process. A candidate asks everyone for votes and support. And he asks people with money for votes and support *and* money. If the campaign is going well, people not only will vote for the candidate, but will speak to their friends about him, and if they can, will make a contribution—and everyone can contribute something. If the campaign is going poorly, a candidate's supporters may still vote for him, but they'll do little else.

At the beginning of the Senate primary race in Oklahoma in 1964, Edmondson and Gary were way ahead of me in the polls. Big givers were not anxious to shower me with cash. But the polls also showed that most voters were still undecided, even though they knew Gary and Edmondson very well. Our job was to convince the undecided. And we started out, with a little money and a lot of faith, to convince them.

It was generally rumored in Oklahoma that the Kerr family was going to bankroll me completely. I didn't discourage this talk, because it helped give me standing as a serious candidate. And I did get some assistance from them, though not nearly so much as I had hoped for, nor anywhere close to what observers believed I was getting. The family did agree to pay the salaries of three staff members who had worked for Senator Kerr in Washington. Two of them were a great help, but we sent one back, because he reacted negatively to every new campaign idea or method, saying, "This is not the way Senator Kerr would have done it." I disagreed with one member of the Kerr family, too, about the choice of a campaign manager. He wanted me to hire a particular man, an experienced old hand, and for a time he made this an absolute condition for supporting me financially. I wanted a close friend, Bill McCandless, a volunteer who had had no experience in Oklahoma politics; I thought this lack of experience was his best asset. After some tense moments, the Kerr family member backed down.

During the campaign, this same Kerr family member arranged a special meeting with me because he was concerned about my wife, LaDonna. Too much attention was being focused on her, he said. In many areas of Oklahoma at that time, particularly in the southern portion of the state, women took little active part in politics. Such behavior was just not proper.

I rejected his advice out of hand. LaDonna and I had grown up in Cotton County, Oklahoma—she a Comanche Indian, I a poor white. We had married when we were only eighteen years old, and both of us had worked to get me through the University of Oklahoma. As they say in Oklahoma, we "tracked well." Our ideas were the same, because we had formed them together. We were—and are—each other's best friends. The Kerr family member was wrong on two counts. LaDonna's presence was good politics; she helped bring the women out to our meetings, and she charmed both them and their husbands. More important for us, we liked being with each other; it made the campaign fun.

Now that I was the Democratic nominee for the Senate, I began to get some money—as Magnuson had promised—from the national Senate Democratic Campaign Committee. The Oklahoma Democratic party and organized labor in the state were also helpful. We could afford to charter a plane, and could therefore cover more ground. The flying, in small planes, was hazardous. The Oklahoma fall weather was often bad, and many of the airports were nothing more than grass strips. There were some close calls.

One time, LaDonna and I and Katherine Hatch, then a reporter for the *Oklahoma City Times,* were flying into Tulsa when our single engine quit. The pilot told us that the problem was carburetor ice and that he would have to make a forced landing in the bed of the Arkansas River. I explained to the women in the back seat how to get out rapidly when we landed, and tried to reassure them. But luckily, just at the last moment, the motor started up again and we were able to continue in the landing pattern and come in safely. To relieve the tension as we got out of the plane, I said to the pilot, jokingly, "Charlie, I've got as much confidence in you as I would have in Wiley Post."

Katherine Hatch, badly shaken, asked if I knew what Will Rogers's last words were. I said I didn't. "They were, 'Wiley Post, you one-eyed son of a bitch!' " she said, and we all laughed, almost hysterically.

Another time, with a different pilot, a campaign aide and I were flying at night from Tulsa to Oklahoma City in impossibly bad weather. It was raining heavily and visibility was extremely poor. The pilot was flying just under the clouds and just above the Tulsa Turnpike, in order to keep his bearings. The clouds kept getting lower, and we kept getting lower. Sometimes, going through a cut in a hill, our plane was lower than the trees on each side of the highway, and oncoming cars would click their dimmers off and on to signal us to dim our landing lights, which the pilot had switched on for better vision. Finally, the pilot gave up and said that he was going to put the craft on the ground. We landed on the turnpike, banging up one wing considerably on a string of roadside reflectors. The aide and I jumped out, stopped the cars behind us, and prepared to push the plane onto the grass shoulder. As luck would have it, the first car to stop was Governor Henry Bellmon's limousine, carrying the governor himself and a number of other passengers. He offered to radio ahead for a highway patrolman to come and help us. The next car was driven by a United Press reporter, who had been following the governor. My pilot, who, I later learned, did not have an instrument rating, whispered to me, "I hope we can keep this out of the press." He didn't know much about news.

Three things figured heavily in my victory over Wilkinson by 22,000 votes: Wilkinson's decision to bring Senator Strom Thurmond of South Carolina to the state, President Johnson's landslide win over Senator Barry Goldwater in the presidential election, and a televised debate between Wilkinson and me.

From the first, it was apparent to everyone that in order to beat Wilkinson, I would—among other things—have to get at least 90 percent of the black vote in the state. All of the state's recognized black leaders supported me, because LaDonna and I had been active in civil-rights causes and because I had pushed through the state legislature a measure banning discrimination in state employment. Wilkinson's way of countering my strength with blacks was to send Prentice Gautt, the first black to play football at the University of Oklahoma, around to all the black areas of the state to show game films and urge a vote for his former coach. And Gautt did have some effect. The first poll we saw reported 40 percent of the black vote going to Wilkinson, 50 percent to me, and 10 percent undecided. If these proportions held, they could be disastrous for us, we knew, because the election promised to be extremely close.

But we didn't know what to do about it. We had not been able to get Wilkinson to express his opinion on civil-rights issues. Luckily, he solved the problem for us, by bringing the Senate's most rabid opponent of civil-rights legislation, Strom Thurmond, to Oklahoma to help out in his campaign. Thurmond was booked for appearances only in the southeastern Oklahoma counties where the race issue was the hottest, and Oklahoma's liberals, black and white, raised a considerable fuss about this fact. After Thurmond's appearances in the state, the polls showed us beating Wilkinson 8 to 2 among black voters. Too, Thurmond had scared the daylights even out of a lot of conservative white voters with his jingoist speeches about Vietnam at a time when President Johnson, particularly as compared with Goldwater, was seeming to promise not to increase our involvement there.

We tied our fall campaign to the president's. Lyndon Johnson was a neighbor, well-known in that part of the country. He talked our language. He was highly popular in Oklahoma—and almost everywhere else as well, it turned out, at least in that election. He carried the state, and the nation, overwhelmingly. For the first time since Harry Truman's smashing upset victory in 1948, a majority of Oklahomans gave their votes to the Democratic candidate for president.

For quite a while, many people in the state who were nominal, registered members of the party had actually been what we called "Yes, but" Democrats: "Yes, I'm a Democrat, but I can't vote for Adlai Stevenson"; or, "Yes, I'm a Democrat, but I can't stand John Kennedy." With a couple of brief lapses, Oklahoma had been a one-party state since it was admitted to the Union in 1907. That one party was the Democratic party, all right, but in its outlook—on race, on government spending, on social programs—it bore little resemblance to the national Democratic party. For years, the true conservative gospel had been preached to Oklahoma's voters by the state's leading newpapers—the *Daily Oklahoman* and the *Oklahoma City Times,* both owned by octogenarian E. K. Gaylord, a right-winger except when good business dictated otherwise; the *Tulsa World,* run by an acquisitive and conservative lawyer, Byron Boone; and the *Tulsa Tribune,* edited by a second-generation world traveler, Jenkin Lloyd Jones, who fancied himself a conservative intellectual.

Oklahoma had not always been conservative. In fact, when it became a state, its constitution, threaded through with Populist principles, was thought to be one of the most liberal state constitutions in the nation. In the earliest years of Oklahoma politics, the Republican party probably ranked fourth in importance, behind not only the Democrats, but the Populists and Socialists as well. Even as late as 1917, police officials in Oklahoma had to use considerable force to put down a draft-resistance movement—the Green Corn Rebellion—led by the Working Class Union, an indigenous organization, resembling the I.W.W., with an integrated membership of radical whites, blacks, and Indians.

But with the coming of oil, Oklahoma's radical political tradition had been lost. Oil interests, and those related to them, backed by the metropolitan newspapers, had increasingly come to dominate state politics. And the conservative voices in Oklahoma had reached their shrillest pitch in 1960, in opposition to the election of John F. Kennedy.

My wife and I had first met Kennedy, then senator from Massachusetts, when he came to an Oklahoma Democratic fundraising luncheon in 1957. After the luncheon, we were among a dozen or so people who were invited up to his hotel room to have a more intimate chat while he munched on a club sandwich. I told a friend later that although I was impressed by Kennedy's youthful dynamism and winning self-assurance, I did not believe he was ready to be nominated for president in 1960. My friend reminded me that I had said very much the same thing, early in the race, about the chances Howard Edmondson had of being elected governor. My friend proved right, of course, and I was wrong.

Kennedy was nominated in 1960, but he was not my choice. Neither was Lyndon Johnson, whom most Oklahoma delegates supported at the Los Angeles convention that year. My heart still belonged to Adlai Stevenson. My wife and I were not delegates to the 1960 convention, but back home in Lawton, by the television set, we kept pulling for the small band of die-hard Stevensonians there. They were led by Senator Mike Monroney of Oklahoma, Eleanor Roosevelt, and others. But, alas, the Stevensonian era had ended, and even a tumultuous popular demonstration when Stevenson had entered the convention hall was unable to slow the Kennedy juggernaut more than momentarily. Kennedy became the nominee, and Johnson his running mate.

In Lawton, Oklahoma, it was hell supporting Kennedy against Nixon. We organized teas to try to make our viewpoint more socially acceptable. We sent delegations to tell the local Baptist preacher that if he continued to denounce Kennedy from his Sunday pulpit, we would pass out leaflets in front of his church. We couldn't sell Kennedy in Oklahoma in 1960, but we were thrilled at his national victory. We were caught up by his inaugural words and by the grace and style of his Presidency.

Like most Americans, I can remember exactly where I was when I heard the shocking news of President Kennedy's assassination. I was eating lunch in the Biltmore Hotel in Oklahoma City with some of the members of my campaign staff. A person coming by our table asked if we had heard that the president had been shot in Dallas. My first reaction was that we were being told another "sick" Kennedy joke; I'd already encountered more than enough of them on the campaign trail throughout Oklahoma. But this report was, sadly, true. It knocked the props out from under us. We temporarily suspended the campaign for the Democratic nomination for the Senate, even though the primary was to be held in about six months. We were shocked and numb, and went home to spend long tearful days in front of our television sets.

Then, Lyndon Johnson rallied the nation, and us. Vietnam and its problems seemed small and far away. And Johnson's conservative opposition was scattered and disorganized in the face of his "Let us continue" call. When he went to the people in the fall of 1964, Johnson was made even more appealing by the comparison to Barry Goldwater. We tied our Senate campaign to his. Our campaign bumper stickers read, "Harris/LBJ." It was a help.

A televised debate with Wilkinson also played a crucial part in my victory. I had not wanted to debate with him, but he kept challenging me, and before long, my supporters were telephoning from all around the state, saying that they were losing the coffee-shop arguments on the question; they didn't know how to respond to the taunts that their candidate was afraid to debate with Wilkinson. So I challenged *him* to a debate—not the kind of joint appearance that he wanted, in which, as on "Meet the Press," we would be questioned together by a panel of newsmen, but a real debate, by college rules, in which each of us would have to stand on his own and make his own case.

By the time of the debate, we had already begun to cut Wilkinson down to size, to deflate his hero image, with humor. The process had started at my big fall kick-off rally in Oklahoma City.

Prior to the rally, a bunch of us had sat around in a hotel room trying to think up funny things to say about Wilkinson, and we began to have such a good time, and laughed so much at our own jokes, that we were late for the rally. Most of the funny things we thought up were too in-house or too far-out. The main one we decided to use on that occasion had to do with the fact that Wilkinson's set speech, which he gave over and over at Rotary Club and chamber of commerce luncheons, centered around the question of why Rome fell. Rome fell, according to Wilkinson, because the people became too dependent on welfare; they gave up their freedom for security. The same thing was happening in America, he said.

That was my theme, then, at the rally in Oklahoma City, opening my campaign there for the general election. "We are a little late in getting this campaign under way, because I found that I was poorly prepared to discuss what has turned out to be the principal issue in this campaign—why Rome fell," I said. "I've had to study up on the question. And I've discovered that the main reason why Rome fell was that the people became so carried away with sports that they decided to let the gladiators help run the government." Bad history, perhaps, but no worse than Wilkinson's.

By debate time, Wilkinson was gradually becoming an ordinary human being in the eyes of most Oklahomans, a football coach who had changed his profession, his name, and his party registration to become a politician. And the debate, as was our plan, made him show his true ideological colors for the first time. He attacked the spendthrift "Socialist" policies of the Democratic party, vigorously endorsed Barry Goldwater, and alienated what little black support he still had left. The debate was the frosting on the cake.

No other candidate in Oklahoma's recent history had ever conducted as intensive a person-to-person campaign as I did for the Senate in 1964. No campaign had ever involved so many volunteers. And on election night it seemed that most of them had come to Oklahoma City for a wild, confetti-throwing victory party in the ornate ballroom of the Biltmore Hotel.

I felt inadequate and somehow insincere in trying to thank

them for their help. Thanks didn't seem enough. I would wake up the next morning and fly to Washington to be sworn in as a senator immediately, since I had been elected to complete an unexpired term. But I knew that most of them would have to return to their everyday lives, let down, perhaps never again to be caught up with such enthusiasm in a cause they thought important and meaningful.

My mood was almost melancholy when I rose to speak that night. Theirs was almost hysterical with happiness. "I don't promise you that in the years ahead, you and I will always agree," I said. "If I agreed with each of you one hundred percent, I would either be dishonest or I'd be a fool. I don't promise you that I'll always be right. I do promise you that I'll always be doing what I *think* is right, and you'll never have to wonder where I stand. I'll never forget you, and I'll never let you down."

LaDonna and I shook the last hands and said our last good-bys and thank yous and went back up to our hotel room with my mother and father. My dad's Mississippi family had come out to Oklahoma as sharecroppers when he was a boy, and he and my mother had had a hard life, economically. My dad was dressed up in an unaccustomed suit, one of my old ones. Both he and my mother had campaigned for me as best they could. She was ecstatic at the thought that her boy was about to become a member of the Senate of the United States; partly to hide his true feelings, my dad made a show of being a little less carried away.

"Well, it's pretty nice, but I can't see that it will improve my credit at the bank any," he said.

3

The Most Exclusive
Men's Club in the World

The late Senator Richard Russell of Georgia remarked to me one time that you can tell by looking at a senator how many years there are remaining in his six-year term. "If he's got six years to go, he's looking up, his thoughts away off somewhere," he said. "If it's about four years until he has to run again, he's looking straight ahead, and if he's in the last two years of his term, he's looking down, watching where he steps."

I came to the Senate of the United States looking down, watching where I stepped. I had been elected to complete an unexpired term, and would come up for re-election in only two years, in 1966. I took the oath of office in Washington the day after I was elected, and was a senator almost before the fact of my victory had had time to register on me fully.

Early in the morning, after our great victory party in Oklahoma City, LaDonna and I and two other couples—Bill and Betty McCandless and Harvey and Jean Porter, our good friends and supporters—caught a plane for the nation's capital. They wanted to see me sworn in.

At the airport in Washington, we were met by Don McBride, who had been a member of Senator Kerr's staff. Our party split up, occupying two cars. McCandless, Porter, and I rode with McBride, and he briefed me on what committee assignments to ask for. He advised me to try to get on one of the "water" committees—the Interior and Insular Affairs Committee or the Public Works Committee—so that I could follow through on Senator Kerr's program for developing Oklahoma's water resources. He said that I should talk personally about obtaining this assignment with Senator Carl Hayden of Arizona, who was the dean of the Senate and an influential member of the Senate Steering Committee, which made committee assignments.

Don McBride had known me as a promising but very young state senator. I was still only thirty-three, the youngest person ever elected to the Senate from Oklahoma. It must have been difficult for Don to get used to the idea that I was to take Senator Kerr's seat. "Fred, what you have to realize is that the Senate is made up of ninety-nine other prima donnas," he said. "I know it's going to be difficult for you to do it at first, but you're going to have to become a prima donna yourself, in order to get along here."

I nudged McCandless and Porter. "It *will* be hard for me, Don," I said, "but I'll do my best." McCandless and Porter broke up. I'm certain that dedicated, somewhat stodgy, Don McBride thought we were not nearly serious enough.

At the office of the secretary of the Senate, Felton M. "Skeeter" Johnston, LaDonna and our friends were asked to wait in the reception room while I was ushered in for a private briefing on the privileges and emoluments of a senator. Johnston, a courtly Southerner who had been a Senate retainer for most of his life, told me that he had served Senator Kerr and Senator Edmondson to the best of his ability and now he would similarly serve me. He called in Robert Brenkworth, the Senate disbursing officer, who was all business in telling me about the insurance and retirement programs. I didn't catch any of it. Brenkworth also launched into a detailed discussion of "clerk-hire," the amount of money I could use for a staff of my own. Showing me a "confidential" table of figures, he explained the "base" allowances for clerk-hire, which, depending on how I allocated them, would translate into higher "actual" salaries. I didn't understand these arrangements then, and I don't now. I never knew why there were two sets of figures, or why they were confidential.

And before I knew it, I had been sworn in. Brenkworth gave me a sheet of paper to sign. It contained an oath to support and defend the Constitution of the United States. He asked me to hold up my hand, recite some words, and say "I do." I did. "Well, you're on the payroll," he said, his job finished. LaDonna and our friends, who had flown thirteen hundred miles to see the culmination of all their work, had missed it. I had hardly been aware of it myself.

But I was a senator, nevertheless, a member of what was called, even then, despite Margaret Chase Smith's membership, "the most exclusive men's club in the world." We walked over to the office Howard Edmondson had occupied in the New Senate Office Building. It was to be mine until a permanent office assignment could be made. Almost immediately, I received a call from an aide to the majority leader, Senator Mike Mansfield of Montana, who wanted me to come to his office in the Capitol right away. The leader wanted to see *me*. Flushed with the excitement of it, I left LaDonna and our friends again and hurried down the corridor to a bank of elevators. One button read, "Senators Only." I decided to use it. The door promptly opened on an elevator that was empty except for a young operator, who looked at me disdainfully, barring my entrance with his arm and searching the hall with his eyes. Then, the operator closed the door. Nothing daunted, as they say, I punched the "Senators Only" button again. I was in a hurry because I had an appointment with the majority leader. Once again, the elevator arrived, and the door opened. But seeing it was me, the same young man, obviously irritated, said, "Sir, can't you read? The sign says, 'Senators Only.' "

This time, I pushed my way onto the elevator before he could close the door. "I *am* a senator," I said, embarrassed. "But, of course, you shouldn't know it; I was just elected."

The young man was even more embarrassed than I. He apologized, and to make up for his error, he asked solicitously, "Would you like a car, sir?" I said I would, although I wasn't sure what he meant, and he pushed a special button on the control console.

By so doing, it turned out, he notified the driver of the trolley which runs underground between the Senate office buildings and the Capitol that a senator was on the way. Sure enough, I saw the trolley waiting when I stepped out of the elevator, still telling the young operator not to be concerned about his mistake. I chose a seat in the rear of the car, and sat down. Nothing happened. After three or four minutes, I was becoming worried about keeping the majority leader waiting, and I was about to speak to the driver about it when he turned to me and said, "I'm sorry to keep you waiting, sir, but there's a senator coming, and I have to hold the car for him." Luckily, another senator *did* finally come, or I might have been there yet. He stepped into the front compartment, which I later learned was reserved for senators only, and at last we started up and whirred down the tunneled track toward the Capitol.

Mansfield wanted to have coffee and get acquainted. That's all. He was a lean, pipe-smoking frontier professor, spare of frame and spare of speech. He had nothing to ask of me, and simply wished to bid me welcome. I found that strange. In the Oklahoma State Senate, a leader would never have missed such an opportunity to talk about serious matters—about "the Program," about voting with him on the organization of the Senate, about what the Republicans were up to. Not Mansfield. Every senator could do as he pleased, he said. Every senator was as important as any other, and obviously had to do whatever his conscience dictated or his constituents demanded. I told him I wanted to be a member of one of the "water" committees. "I hope it works out," he said, and puffed on his pipe again. That was the most I could get out of him.

But if nothing else was accomplished during this meeting, I did make the acquaintance of Robert Kennedy, who had just been elected senator from New York. He was in Washington for the day, and had been invited over by Mansfield, as had Joseph Montoya, the newly elected senator from New Mexico. We all chatted together, a little woodenly, drinking the terrible coffee which had been poured by the elderly and obsequious black butler. Mansfield sent for a photographer, whose flash caught us as we were at that moment. Mansfield with pipe in mouth. Montoya and me with slicked-back, dark hair. And boyish, short-haired Robert Kennedy.

I barely had time to tell LaDonna and our friends, back at the office, about meeting Robert Kennedy in person before I had to hurry away again, to see Senator Hayden about committee assignments. His office was in the high-ceilinged Old Senate Office Building, where each room had a fireplace. I decided, right then, that I wanted to have my own office there, rather than in the aseptically lavish New Senate Office Building, with its polished red-granite halls, flavorless green carpeting, and characterless, modern walnut paneling. Later, I did get assigned to the Old Senate Office Building. So did Robert Kennedy, who caused a great stir by promptly lighting a fire in one of his fireplaces. It turned out that the beautiful fireplaces no longer worked. Their chimneys had been sealed up, and they had been ducted-in as a part of the air-conditioning system. Kennedy's aromatic oak-wood smoke quickly spread throughout the building.

Senator Hayden had been a member of Congress since the first day of Arizona's statehood. Before that, he'd been a county sheriff, and he'd campaigned for Congress at stagecoach stations. He sat behind a massive, antique walnut desk which looked older than he did, if that was possible. To his left, was an ornate, greenish travertine fireplace. He was a big-boned man, with his weathered skin stretched tight against his bones. He seemed ancient and hairless—with no eyebrows and little top hair. But there was a faint light of merriment in his eyes and a hint of a smile around the corners of his thin lips. A couple of years later, responding to a *Time* magazine story which said, "Aging old Senator Hayden of Arizona dottered into the Senate," he announced, "I don't dotter; I *shuffle.*"

I took a seat in front of his desk and launched into my pitch about wanting to be on one of the "water" committees. As I talked, Senator Hayden's eyelids closed, and his face relaxed into an expressionless repose. My Lord, he's gone to sleep on me! I thought, and I cut my presentation short. But the moment I stopped talking, his eyes opened again. He sat up in his chair and said in a surprisingly firm voice, "All right, son, I'll help you get on either the Public Works Committee or the Interior Committee, and once you're on one or the other, I want you to vote for my Central Arizona Water Project." He hadn't been asleep at all. I told him I would vote for his project.

Senator Hayden gave me some advice about campaigning for re-election, too. "Do like I do," he said. "Just shake hands with 'em and give 'em a card. If they want to talk about issues, just listen and then say that you're glad to see 'em, and move on to the next person.

"When you're dealing with the press," he went on, "don't talk more than you have to. They can't quote silence."

I knew that this was probably good advice. But I knew too that it was not of much use to a talker like me.

On my first day as a senator, I also got a free haircut in the senators' private barbershop in the Capitol. LaDonna and I and our friends wanted to go on to New York for a celebration holiday, and the campaigning of the last few weeks had left no time for me to get my hair trimmed. I knew that senators had their own barbershop because I'd read about it. I called, and the shop was open. Three barbers in white uniforms and white shoes greeted me respectfully when I came through the unmarked swinging doors. Each stood behind his own chair until I had chosen one and sat down. A black shine man slid his stand over at once and began to apply polish to my shoes, as the barber went to work with his scissors and comb. "Senator, I'm going to leave it a little full on the sides," the barber said. "It photographs better." He was right, it turned out.

I tipped the barber a dollar and gave a quarter to the shine man, who, when I stood up to leave, brushed off my coat and helped me on with it. "Let me show you something before you go," my barber said, opening a high walnut cabinet which stood against one wall. Inside, were rows and rows of old-fashioned shaving mugs, of white china with real gold trim. On the front of each was the beautifully lettered name of a senator. "One of these will be made up for you," the barber said. "And if you quit or get beat, you get to take it with you." I couldn't imagine having a shave in a barbershop (and I never did). Quitting or getting beat wasn't very much on my mind either, that first day in the Senate; still, it seemed a quaintly nice touch to be furnished with your very own shaving mug with your name on it.

By the time the Senate came back into session in January, 1965, my Senate office had long been going full swing and was already a month behind in answering the mail. The mail! It started coming almost the moment I was sworn in, and it came twice a day. And it kept coming. In volume, my mail was at least double that of my Senate colleague from Oklahoma, Mike Monroney. I was fresh from a campaign, and people had believed me when I said that I would be interested in their problems and their views. I got word of both their problems and their views at the rate of about three hundred letters a day. For the first year, I tried to read every piece of incoming mail, and I signed every piece of outgoing mail. I lived in dread that I might—for example—send a letter beginning "Dear Mr. Wilson" to an old friend I had for years been calling "Charley." The mail dogged my steps. It followed me home in a cardboard box every night. It went with me when I presided over the Senate. And for all that painstaking personal attention, I began to hear repeated complaints about how long it took to get an answer from me, weeks longer than to get one from Monroney, it was said.

Vice-President Hubert Humphrey had advised me never to send out a letter that didn't read the way it would if I had answered it in person. "The mail is enormously important; make your answers as personal as you can," he said. We tried. Lord, how we tried! But when we began to run more than a month behind, we finally had to give up. Bill Carmack, a university professor and communications expert who had come to Washington with me as my administrative assistant, talked with staff members of other senators and devised a new mail system for us. A staff member would open the incoming letters and assign each of them, depending on the subject matter, to one of the other staff members, who would draft a response for my signature. Stock paragraphs were written up for use by the secretaries whenever appropriate. Arrangements were made with the "robo room," downstairs, to robotype—that is, have typed by the electric robot typewriters—form letters to serve as answers to the mail on certain recurring topics. Letters of this sort could not be distinguished from those personally typed. There was even an electric machine, which I didn't use much, that could sign a letter in ink with an exact duplicate of my signature. The whole arrangement was necessary but disconcerting. On my visits to Oklahoma twice a month, I was always being asked by someone whether or not I had received the letter he or she had written me. "Yes, and we're working on it," was the stock reply. I never liked it.

Bill Carmack said that the only way to comply with Humphrey's advice, to make our letters sound as they would if we were answering in person, would be to change the way we *talked*—to talk in what we called "letterese." "How are you, this morning?" a person on the street might ask. The letterese response would be: "Thank you very much for the question contained in your communication. We have referred your question to the appropriate government agency, and you may be sure that we will be back in touch with you as soon as we have received their response. Please do not hesitate to let me know if I can be of further assistance to you in any way." Much the same response would work, whether the person had asked about a Social Security claim or about how to avoid the draft.

But if many of our letters were forms, we really did concentrate on "case work," on helping those who had written about personal problems with the government. We thought of our office as that of an ombudsman, a sort of last resort for people who could think of no other place to turn. And most other members of Congress had the same attitude. Case work, we felt, made our huge government halfway workable for individual citizens, and it sometimes exposed weaknesses or inequities in the laws and ultimately brought about changes in them.

We paid a lot of attention to "issue mail," too, although most of it was answered with stock paragraphs. Senators do not worry only about the views of the majority of their constituents. They also keep a wary eye out for active minorities, who feel strongly enough about an issue to raise money to defeat a senator or to help field a strong candidate against him. In our office, we didn't count the mail or weigh it, but it was, nevertheless, one of the barometers we used to gauge back-home opinion; however, we got awfully tired of some "pen pals" who wrote us once or twice a week, and we hardly bothered to read form letters that were obviously the result of some organized lobbying drive. Now and again, we would get a well-reasoned, carefully drafted letter which furnished us with information and sound arguments, and that's what we were always short on.

I wouldn't want to be on a senator's staff. The Senate was characterized by a rigid caste system. To be sure, personal secretaries and administrative assistants—the so-called AAs'—ranked above other staff members, but all were regarded as separate from and lower than the senators. All called their boss *"the Senator,"* in a tone even more respectful than that of a nurse as she says, *"Doctor* will see you now." Senators and their staffs seldom socialized together, except at somewhat embarrassed, semiformal occasions, such as Christmas parties, when the boss was presented with the staff's gift of a new set of luggage and a card, signed by everybody, that said, "We'll keep working, so you can keep traveling." The member of a senator's staff seldom got to know any other senator personally, and *never* became really friendly with one. They were stopped by the caste barrier. The staffs of senators who were well known and in the news looked down on the staffs of senators who were less well known. And if you were a staff member, it didn't matter whether you were a brilliant writer, a meticulous researcher, or an aggressive case worker; the outside world would probably never know it. Your job was to serve *your* senator, to keep him pleased and in office.

Our office was somewhat different, in that the people I brought to Washington with me were my friends, and they remained my friends, the ones LaDonna and I saw most often. But I worried about what the caste system did to them. I was appalled, for example, when I first saw a Senate staff office—jam-packed with four or five desks to a room, each staff member trying to do his or her work in a crowded, unpartitioned arena that sounded, when everybody was on the phone at the same time, like a cattle auction.

Senators had their own gymnasium; staff members had none. Senators had two semiprivate dining rooms and one totally private dining room; staff members lined up in the public cafeteria. Senators could get away from it all at will, by going to their own off-limits inner sanctum, the Marble Room, a chandelier-hung, plush chamber off the Senate floor, furnished with leather couches, stuffed pillows, and reclining chairs, and stocked with all the hometown newspapers; staff members could never get away, even for a moment, from the mail, the telephones, and the constituents. While senators had their own private barbershop, staff members were run, like sheep at shearing time, through a basement staff shop operated by bored civil-service barbers.

A competent and proud young staff member of mine, Gary Dage, son of Don Dage, was incensed about the way he was treated around the Senate, particularly in the staff barbershop, where they didn't even brush the hair off your clothes after they'd finished, he said. He vowed he'd shame his barber the next time he went there, by making a big show of brushing himself off. But even that didn't turn out well. As he and Bill Carmack told me later, Gary got up out of the chair in his shirt sleeves and raised one arm, preparing to brush the hair off his own shirt ostentatiously. But, alas, on the first sweep, Gary's hand caught on a fountain pen in his shirt pocket, and in full view of everyone, the bemused barber included, he ripped the pocket off his shirt. So much for staff demonstrations.

I didn't hire a speech writer at first, and I should have. In the beginning, it never occurred to me that I'd need one. In the Oklahoma State Senate, a senator was expected to rise and speak to the always-full chamber on the spur of the moment. He was expected to know his subject and to be able to express his views with persuasive force. Debate meant something. It changed minds. Senators waited to decide about their votes until they had heard the debate. Not so in the United States Senate. Speeches were pre-written and read to an empty chamber, or, more frequently, were handed to the clerk to be printed in the *Congressional Record*, as if they had been read. That was a shock to me. Some years later, on a visit to the British Parliament, I asked a member of the House of Commons how many staff members he had. He said he had none, and asked how many I had. I said I had twenty-one. "Whatever do they all do?" he asked, astonished. I told him that they answered mail, did research, handled constituents' requests, and wrote speeches. "Write speeches!" he declared, doubly amazed. "Do you mean to say that senators rise on the floor of the Senate and read what someone else has written? Why, even the prime minister himself has only a very few personal staff members. One would think it an outrage, here in the Commons, if a member were unable to rise and argue his own case."

But in eight years in the U.S. Senate, I never knew debate to affect votes, except for one time, in 1966, when Edmund Muskie of Maine spoke for the Model Cities bill. I always wished there were some way to change things, so that debate would be of real consequence in the Senate, but I could never figure out how to do it. Until Assistant Majority Leader Robert Byrd of West Virginia managed to have the rule tightened, Senate speeches did not even have to be germane to the subject under consideration. That change in the rules helped. And Byrd has also advocated that Senate sessions be televised. I believe that's a good idea. It would pull senators to the floor when the Senate was in session, and would put them on their best behavior.

I could never figure out, either, how to become less dependent on staff. Time for reading and reflection was almost nonexistent for most senators. You had to learn orally—from lobbyists, good and bad, from staff members, from witnesses in committee hearings. But committee hearings turned out to be more "show" than tell—the senators' show. There were too many committees and subcommittees, always meeting at the same time. And there were always ten or fifteen unanswered telephone calls waiting, visiting constituents who couldn't be ignored, roll-call votes in the Senate chamber, and breakfasts, lunches, and dinners sponsored by convening national organizations and attended by delegates from back home eager for their senator to join them. Senator Jennings Randolph of West Virginia advised me that I should attend all of my committee and subcommittee hearings every single day, and ask at least one question at each meeting. That way, he said, my attendance would be a matter of record.

So, like most senators, harried and distracted, scooting from one meeting to another, I would come into a committee hearing in progress, get a quick, whispered briefing from the staff member who had been covering the hearing for me before I arrived, and ask the witness of the moment a question or two, sometimes written out and handed to me by my staff member. And then, making my ritualistic senatorial "conflicting committee meeting" apology to the chairman, who understood very well because he did the same thing himself when he was not presiding, I would take my leave.

I was assigned, as I had requested, to the Public Works Committee—one of the "water" committees—and to the Government Operations Committee, which had oversight jurisdiction over all federal agencies. John McClellan, my neighbor from Arkansas, a solemn, strait-laced Senate patriarch, had asked me to become a member of the Government Operations Committee, which he chaired. He liked me. Vice-President Humphrey too had advised me to seek assignment to the Government Operations Committee. "It's a good place to learn about the federal government," he said, "and you can move up fast, because a lot of senators leave it for more prestigious committees when they've built up a little seniority." He also said that every former senator who had become president had served on that committee.

The most powerful committees in the Senate, and hence those to which assignment is most desired, are Appropriations, Finance, Foreign Relations, and Armed Services. Freshman Senators generally can't become members of one of these, right off. But Majority Leader Mansfield had instituted a rule that new senators would get at least one "good" subcommittee assignment. Mine was Public Works. I soon wished that I had asked for Education and Welfare or Judiciary. They dealt with much more important questions, and, too, on those committees, each majority member—that is, each member belonging to the party forming the majority in the Senate—was automatically made chairman of his own committee. Thus he gained something useful to do, a greater chance to make a mark, and a good deal more staff.

The U.S. Congress differs from the Oklahoma State Senate, and from every other major parliamentary body, in that committee heads are chosen purely on the basis of seniority. If senators live and are re-elected, and if those with greater seniority die or get beat or quit, they will inexorably move up. The saying around the Senate was, "When I first came to the Senate, I didn't think much of the seniority system, but the longer I stay here, the better I like it." Each Senate committee was run by its chairman like a powerful barony. He alone chose the majority staff; the ranking minority member chose the minority staff. The chairman alone decided what bills would be taken up, and when. He alone decided when, and if, hearings would be held on a measure which had been referred to the committee, and when the committee would get around to holding "mark-up" sessions to decide on a bill's final form.

In my very first mark-up session as a member of the Public Works Committee, I got off to what I was later told was a "very bad start with the chairman," the late Senator Pat McNamara of Michigan. Mark-up sessions were closed to the press and the public. This one had been called to decide upon the final form of a relatively minor bill. Two long, rectangular tables had been pushed end to end in the committee room. The chairman sat at one end. Republican members of the committee sat along one side, Democrats along the other. Ranking lowest in seniority, I was down at the foot, farthest from the chairman. He almost needed a telescope to see me. I had come prepared to offer an amendment to one of the bill's sections, but when that section was reached in the course of the committee's deliberations, the chairman simply announced that he thought it was all right in its present form, and without asking if there were any comments or objections, started to move on to the next section.

"Excuse me just a moment, Mr. Chairman," I spoke up from my end of the table, "I have an amendment I would like to offer to that section." Committee staff members jumped with surprise. All heads turned toward me. Chairman McNamara looked up as if he couldn't quite tell where the strange and discordant voice had come from. "I have an amendment I would like to offer to that section," I repeated, so that he could zero in on me.

"Yes, well—," the chairman began, obviously a little at a loss as to who I was. An aide whispered in his ear. "Yes, well—Harris, isn't it? Well, I think the committee is fairly well satisfied with that section, the way it is."

"Nevertheless, I would like to have my amendment read and have a chance to explain it," I said. I was nervous but persistent.

"Very well," he said, irritated. The clerk read my amendment, and I briefly explained its purpose. When I'd finished, the chairman said, "I still don't think we need it. We'll go on through the rest of the bill, and then, if you want to press your amendment, we'll come back to that section." But we didn't. Instead, after the committee had considered the remainder of the bill, the chairman simply announced that he was ready for a motion to report the bill to the Senate.

"Mr. Chairman," I said.

"Yes, what is it?" he asked, as if I had not spoken earlier.

I told him that I still wanted to press my amendment. He asked whether I wanted a vote on it, and I said I did. He was annoyed at the delay, sure that the vote would be futile. By that time, I too thought it would probably be futile, since no other committee member had spoken up in my support. But when the vote was taken, I won. My amendment was adopted. I was as surprised as the chairman.

Irascible but goodhearted, old Senator McNamara never tried to punish me in any way for my impertinence—partly, I think, because he could never remember my name.

Senator John McClellan of Arkansas, on the other hand, knew

my name well. We came from adjoining states, and shared a common interest in the taming and development of the Arkansas River, which ran through both our states. Senator Kerr had been his great friend and collaborator in the Senate, and I was uncomfortable with the fact that McClellan thought of me as another Bob Kerr. Many other people on the national scene also thought of me in that way. For example, an early story about me in the *New York Herald Tribune* said, "Fred Harris is rapidly becoming the new Bob Kerr of the Senate for his ability to work well with others and get difficult things done." I knew I was *not* going to become a new Bob Kerr, but, right at first, I wasn't totally sure what I *was* going to become.

I appreciated McClellan's friendship and his almost fatherly interest in me. I was honored when he made me a member of his antiracketeering and anticorruption Permanent Investigating Subcommittee. I was grateful when, at my suggestion, he created the new Subcommittee on Government Research in my first year in the Senate and appointed me chairman of it. But I was troubled from the first by the way the Investigating Subcommittee sometimes badgered witnesses, and McClellan and I slowly drifted apart. The big rift came much later, during our investigation of the causes of black riots. McClellan was totally convinced that the riots had been the result of a massive conspiracy. I was equally convinced that their causes were much deeper. So, at the beginning of one Senate session, McClellan simply announced that he had reduced the membership of the Permanent Investigating Subcommittee. It had been too large and unwieldy, he said, but it happened that the reduction left no place on it for me. At the same time, McClellan told me that in order to hold down the budget of the Government Operations Committee, he would have to eliminate my Subcommittee on Government Research. I didn't mind leaving the Investigating Subcommittee. I did hate losing my own subcommittee and having to discharge its staff. But there was no recourse.

I had come to the Senate less than adequately prepared on two principal subjects: economics and foreign policy. My closest friends among the new members of the Senate, Walter "Fritz" Mondale of Minnesota and Robert Kennedy of New York, had had long-time exposure to both. Fritz Mondale had been an early national officer of Students for Democratic Action, had traveled abroad, was a close associate of Hubert Humphrey's, and had been a worker since high-school days in the liberal Democratic Farmer-Labor party in Minnesota. Bob Kennedy was Washington-wise, well staffed and well informed. He had served in his late brother's cabinet, taking a large role in almost every area of government policy making. I admired my friends' knowledge of the issues and their self-assurance in dealing with them.

I undertook to educate myself. I read every economics book I could get my hands on. I made an effort to talk with every visiting economist who came through Washington. Sometimes I felt that the more I learned about the "dismal science," the less I knew. But when I later became much more interested in the distribution of wealth and income than in mere government manipulation of fiscal and monetary policy alone, the fact that I had never been totally committed to standard economic practice was probably an asset.

My first two trips outside the country provided quicker education. In 1965, LaDonna and I made a tour of Latin American countries with Senator Birch Bayh of Indiana and his wife, Marvella. And, in late 1966, Senator Henry Jackson of Washington, chairman of the Subcommittee on National Security and International Organizations, on which I served, sent me to a meeting in Wiesbaden, Germany, where the future of the North Atlantic Treaty Organization was to be discussed.

In Latin America, I learned as much about the United States as I did about the countries we visited. We met with dissident students everywhere, and wondered about the lack of comparable activism among our own students, a state of affairs which was even then beginning to change. We walked the slums—the *barriadas* of Lima and the *favelas* of Rio—and compared them to our own. We thought what a shame it was that no real headway had been made in Latin America toward the two principal goals of President Kennedy's Alliance for Progress—tax reform and land reform—until we remembered what little headway had been made toward the same goals in the United States.

Everywhere in Latin America, on that trip, we were confronted with the bitter legacy of hostility toward the United States left by corporate and governmental imperialism of the past. Our own officials, we found, were often uninformed or out of touch. In Guatemala, a country where half the population consisted of Indians who did not speak the official language, Spanish, who were outside the money economy, and who were barely living at the subsistence level, we had a long talk with our own ambassador. I told him that it appeared to me that there was a classic revolutionary situation in Guatemala.

"Not at all," he said, almost cheerily. He was a career diplomat, and he spoke to us as if we were naïve school children. "You see, here, the Indians are not like the Indians in the United States; they are passive and docile. From Spanish colonial days, and before, they have been accustomed to taking orders."

I told him that this sounded a good deal like what the white people in Selma, Alabama, must have been saying about the black people, just before the demonstrations against discrimination there. I said that it seemed to me that the one thing Americans ought to have learned from studying their own history was that downtrodden people will rise. "Not in Guatemala," he said.

But that very day, in the first village we visited, we found that the Indians had refused to do their customary free work on the local roads; it was the first time any such refusal had occurred since the Spanish conquest. And that very night, guerillas took over a Guatemala City radio transmitter and held it for several hours, playing a pro-Castro and anti-American tape recording. Tragically, later on, that same ambassador was kidnaped and killed by guerillas.

In Chile, we met with Christian Democrat Eduardo Frei, the cultivated president of the country. "You North Americans invented public relations, but you are the world's worst practitioners of it," he told us. Our own embassy people in Chile invited LaDonna and me to help dedicate a new village in southern Chile which had been built with United States aid. They drafted a brief speech for me to deliver in Spanish, and they warned us against calling the local people "Indians." That would be an insult to them, the officials said. They couldn't have been more wrong! At the dedication ceremony, I took a chance and interjected a sentence of my own. "My wife is an Indian, a member of the Comanche tribe," I said in Spanish. The crowd absolutely erupted in wild cheering and applause. Later, at lunch, we drank many fervent toasts together and traded Indian songs, and then La-Donna and I left in a fever of embraces all around, and open tears.

My high-school Spanish began to come back to me on this first trip to Latin America, but not nearly well enough or rapidly enough. One morning, outside Tlaxcala, Mexico, we went with some United States embassy officials to visit a farmers' co-operative. Its president had been one of Pancho Villa's old "Golden Boys." He wore leather sandals, a huge straw sombrero, a white blouse, and loose white trousers cinched at the waist with a wide red sash. A drooping gray mustache dominated his strong brown face. While the embassy officials were trying to work out where the other members of the party would ride, LaDonna and I waited in the back seat of one of the cars, alone with the old man, who, we had been told, spoke no English. After a while, the silence in the car became a little oppressive, and I decided to speak to the old man. Drawing on what I remembered of my high-school Spanish, I took considerable pains to think out the proper grammar and the proper pronunciation for the sentence I was putting together. At last, I turned to the old man and asked, in Spanish, "How long have you been president of the co-operative, sir?" But there was no response from him at all. He sat looking straight ahead, unblinking. The old fellow's hard of hearing, I thought. So I spoke again, this time in a louder voice, still in my remembered Spanish. "How long have you been president of the co-operative, sir?"

He turned to me and in broken English said, apologetically, "I'm sorry; I do not comprehend English." It was clear I still had a way to go in polishing up my Spanish.

If my Spanish was poor, my German was nonexistent. When I

was in Wiesbaden for the NATO meeting, I found it terribly frustrating to talk through interpreters, doubly so because German seemed to me so much like English. I kept telling myself that if I would just pay stricter attention, I would understand what was being said. But it didn't work. One evening in Wiesbaden, on a short walk from my hotel, I passed the beautiful old opera house there, which had somehow survived Allied bombs. I am a music lover, and my tastes are eclectic; I like everything from country music to opera. My favorite opera at that time was *Carmen,* and I noticed that it was being advertised on a poster in front of the opera house. At the top of the poster was the word *Heute.* Latin and Spanish should have helped me, but I wasn't thinking. I didn't know whether *Heute* meant "coming," or "next week," or "today," or what. Back at the hotel, I wrote the word, as I remembered it, on a piece of paper and asked the concierge what it meant. But I had transposed the *e* and the *u.* "Yes, *Huete,* the concierge said helpfully, repeating the word as I had written it. "That means 'hut.' "

Well, it didn't mean "hut" at all. Spelled correctly, it meant "today," as I discovered when I looked out of my hotel window at nightfall and saw white-tied men and long-gowned women going into the opera house. I skipped the NATO conference reception that evening, and enjoyed a great performance of *Carmen,* even though in German it didn't sound to me nearly so smooth and beautiful as in the French to which I was accustomed.

But I learned far more than a new German word on that first trip abroad. I learned that institutions are kept rigid and unchanging, long after anyone can convincingly explain why they should not change, by their founders' pride in authorship and by some kind of self-important bureaucratic inertia. All of the original NATO nations, except France, were represented at the conference, which was presided over by Prince Bernhard of the Netherlands. Virtually all of the delegates from the other countries, and most of the delegates from the United States, including David Rockefeller and John J. McCloy, had been supporters of NATO from its inception. Many had helped in the writing of the original charter. United Auto Workers president Walter Reuther, *New*

York Times correspondent Max Frankel, and I proved to be the troublemakers at the conference. France had ended its military participation in NATO. Most of the remaining members were not putting up their fair share of its costs. There were new opportunities to be grasped for openings to the Soviet Union and Eastern Europe, and many important things that needed doing in the world besides concentrating solely on the military containment of Communism. Reuther, Frankel, and I said that NATO could not effectively continue as a military apparatus alone, and that the charter, fortunately, provided for broader activities. We said that the member nations, in concert, should use NATO for probing the possibilities for détente with the Soviet Union, for resolving certain of their own economic and other problems, and for cooperative efforts in responding to the needs of the Third World.

After one of my brief but impassioned speeches along those lines, I experienced my first encounter with the Oxford debating technique—telling, but not persuasive. "I would say to the senator," one of the British delegates responded, "that when one's boat is leaking, I rather think it is not a good time to take on additional passengers." But the conference didn't know how to fix the leak, either. And Reuther, Frankel, and I remained a distinct minority.

Back in Washington, Senator Jackson, who was one of the coldest of the cold warriors, was a little disappointed, I think, about my newly articulated ideas concerning NATO. But he remained friendly and helpful to me during my early years in the Senate, although, I'm sure, he thought I was awfully naïve in my somewhat "soft" views.

Liberals held a clear majority in the Senate when I became a member in 1964. But they could seldom vote their strength. The conservative Republicans (among whom most of the Republicans could be numbered) and Southern Democrats were able to have their way much of the time. There was a saying around the Senate that "the conservatives will allow the liberals to say 'what,' so long as the conservatives get to say 'how much.' " The liberals could say "public housing," for example, so long as the conservatives got to say "very little."

The conservatives' strength in the Senate was greater than their numbers for several reasons. They were organized and uncompromising. They studied their lessons. They were always on the job, all day and every day. Membership in the Senate was usually their whole life, the pinnacle of their ambitions.

On the other hand, many liberals spoke to a larger, national constituency. Some were working toward nomination for president. Some sought to mobilize public pressure against Senate intransigence. Many had to spend a great deal of their time on the paid lecture circuit, to make financial ends meet.

I came to the Senate from a successful law practice and was in pretty fair shape financially, but that situation didn't last long. The salary was first $32,500, then $37,500, then $42,500. This sounds like a lot. But I hadn't realized that a senator received a "gross" salary, out of which heavy expenses had to be paid. Important constituents had to be entertained when they came to Washington, for example, and even the cost of small luncheons in the senators' dining room, four or five times a month, built up into a sizable figure. There was no allowance for that.

There was an allowance for telegrams and long-distance telephone calls, but in my first years in the Senate it was far from adequate; the actual expenditures ran $3,500 to $4,000 a year above the allowance.

During much of the time I was in the Senate, LaDonna and I maintained two fully furnished homes, one in Oklahoma and one in Washington. Senator Monroney had sold his house in Oklahoma, but this act was greatly criticized, and contributed to his image as one who had gone off to Washington and lost touch with his home state.

The biggest expense item was travel between Washington and Oklahoma. A single one-way coach ticket cost nearly two hundred dollars. In the first years, I was allowed six round trips. But I actually went home at least twenty-four times a year. LaDonna always went with me, and there was no allowance at all for her.

I found that the Senate salary melted away quickly. I had no outside income, no investments. I had resigned from my law firm when I was elected to the Senate; I couldn't see how a senator could practice law without running into severe ethical questions.

And so, as we used to say down home, I had a champagne appetite and a beer income.

Vice-President Humphrey advised me that the only way to pay the bills was to go on the college lecture circuit, which is the modern Chautauqua. He said, too, that a little extra time after each lecture, spent informally with students and faculty members, would pay valuable dividends in the form of new ideas. At first, I was not in much demand, but little by little, the number of lecture invitations began to build up, and I accepted many of them. So did a good number of my liberal colleagues.

The result was that during their free time many liberal senators were *away* from the Senate. The conservatives spent much of their free time together. They not only had the advantage of the seniority system, which had placed them in control of the Senate machinery and most of the important Senate committees. They not only had the advantage of the filibuster rule, which allowed a minority to thwart the will of the majority. They also had vital information, and they shared it with each other. Committee chairmen regularly held back lengthy bills and reports approved by their committees and only had them printed and distributed at the last moment, just before they were to be taken up in the full Senate. But the conservatives knew in advance when a particular piece of legislation would be coming to the Senate floor for consideration, and they could line up their troops.

Majority leader Mansfield, himself a liberal, saw his role as that of a shepherd, rather than a drover. Perhaps reacting to the notorious arm-twisting tactics of his predecessor in the leader's job, Lyndon Johnson, Mansfield never tried to organize the votes on any measure. Senator Eugene McCarthy of Minnesota once told me that Johnson's main trouble had been that although he liked to pose as a farmer and rancher, he didn't really know much about farming and was, therefore, unable to distinguish between the characteristics of various kinds of livestock. "Johnson never knew the difference between hogs and cattle," McCarthy said. "House members are like cattle, and you can drive cattle; the harder you rush them, the better. Senate members, on the other hand, are like hogs, and you have to handle hogs gently; if you try to push them too hard, move them along too rapidly, they'll spook on you and turn around and run back between your legs."

Senator Mansfield seldom made a preannouncement to the Senate of exactly when particular bills or amendments would be called up for consideration, or when votes would be taken. The result was that liberals lost a good many close votes that they should have won.

We once tried to form a liberal caucus in the Senate, to meet one day a week. Senator Lee Metcalf of Montana and Senator Eugene McCarthy led the effort. Years earlier, as members of the House of Representatives, they had helped form the powerful liberal Democratic Study Group there. But this similar effort in the Senate failed, mainly because we could never get the same ten senators at two meetings in succession.

What I missed most in the United States Senate was the kind of informal socializing among colleagues which had been the key element in getting things done in the Oklahoma State Senate. Mansfield was just not the kind of person who enjoyed what he called "chitchat" over a beer or a bourbon, and everyone else was simply too busy. Contact on the Senate floor was brief and hurried, because no one every stayed there very long. I studied the Senate, and senators, by presiding over that body more than anyone else, taking advantage of a job that was considered to be freshman drudgery. And I saw quite a bit of Robert Kennedy and Fritz Mondale, both socially and on the Senate floor, where we sat together.

Senate desks and Senate offices are assigned purely on the basis of seniority. When a vacancy occurs, the desk and the office are offered, separately, to each senator in turn, starting at the top of the seniority list. The reassignment procedure can sometimes take months.

Certain offices are desirable because they are relatively close to the elevators—important when a senator has to rush to the Senate floor for a vote—or to the rooms where committee meetings are held. Certain desks are coveted because of their location on the floor of the Senate. Generally, the higher a senator ranks in seniority, the closer his desk will be to the front. But some desks are desirable because they are on an aisle or near a door, and are therefore more easily accessible. Some senators choose desks because they can be seen from the press gallery or from the family gallery.

Some Senate desks are coveted for their historical importance. Those of Henry Clay, John C. Calhoun, and Daniel Webster are the most sought after. Senator Russell Long of Louisiana occupies the desk that was his mother's when she briefly succeeded his assassinated father, Huey P. Long. Earlier, Russell Long sat at his father's desk, which had also once been Henry Clay's, but he gave it up to Senator Sam Ervin of North Carolina, in order, it was rumored at the time, to tie down Ervin's vote in his race for majority whip of the Senate.

In the drawer of each Senate desk there is carved the name of every senator who ever sat there. The most important name in the drawer of the desk to which I was first assigned was that of Warren G. Harding. I could have wished for a more auspicious beginning.

The Senate is a place of history, and I avidly soaked it up and studied it. I studied, too, as best I could, how the modern Senate worked, how decisions were made, though it wasn't always easy to know for sure. By and large, I believed in the advice most often heard in the Senate: "To get along, you must go along." And I kept one eye on Oklahoma all the time, because I had to stand for re-election just two years after taking office.

The first vote that caused me a lot of political trouble in Oklahoma involved prayer in the public schools. I agreed with a Supreme Court ruling that prohibited a state or a school board from requiring or establishing prayer in the public schools. It seemed to me that freedom of religion, or nonreligion, was a constitutional right that ought not be tampered with. Everett Dirksen, the colorful and wily old minority leader of the Senate, thought otherwise.

Dirksen was at once a personal delight and a public outrage. People forgave him the fact that his law firm in tiny Pekin, Illinois, represented all manner of big oil companies and big drug companies that were affected by Senate decisions. His melodious and marvelously expressive, raspy voice, his shock of gray hair, his puckish humor, and his florid sentences were famous—and loved—throughout the country. Over the years, he had developed into a kind of delightful caricature of himself, and he enjoyed every minute of his own performance. Once, when I was presiding over the Senate, I watched with both pleasure and dismay as he defeated an amendment to provide extra training funds for an antipoverty program. The spectacle was excellent, but the result was terrible. He took as his text an agency statement that mentioned "truck driving" and "ballet dancing" as two of the skills whose teaching would be financed with the new funds. He asked us to visualize little sixteen-year-old girls learning to drive huge diesel trucks. And then, to the uproarious entertainment of a packed gallery and of the senators on the floor, Dirksen, tall, stoop-shouldered and a little heavy, lifted the hem of an imaginary tutu and spun around behind his desk in a too-dainty pirouette, almost falling over his chair, to illustrate how big, burly eighteen-year-old boys would be taught the fine points of ballet.

Dirksen lost the Senate vote on changing the Constitution to allow so-called "voluntary" prayer in the public schools, but not before he had caused enormous difficulties back home on the issue for a number of his fellow senators, myself included. In the 1966 election, my opponent was a little-known businessman named Pat Patterson. He said I was a rubber stamp for Lyndon Johnson, calling me "Little Lyndon from Lawton," and he attacked me as a big spender. But those tactics didn't have much effect. What hurt was the "prayer in the schools" issue. Patterson ran a tough radio commercial on the subject of my prayer vote. The commercial began with the voice of a little girl reciting the Lord's Prayer, while the wail of a police siren, faint at first, grew louder and louder in the background. Then, there was the sound of tires screeching as a car braked, and a firm voice interrupted the little girl's prayer, saying, "Stop! Fred Harris voted to prevent our children from praying in the schools. Vote for Pat Patterson, Republican for United States Senate."

Nevertheless, I won re-election fairly handily. And I came back to the Senate, looking up.

4

The World's Greatest
Deliberative Body

What does it take to be a good senator? That question always reminded me of a question my uncle used to put to me, as to whether they had to pay me to be good, or whether I was good for nothing. And of something Will Rogers said: "It is not the initial cost of a Senator we have to look out for, it's the upkeep." And of the declaration by James Madison that, being a young man and desirous of increasing his reputation as a statesman, he could not afford to accept a seat in the Senate.

But it's a serious question, one about which I sometimes sought other opinions. Vice-President Humphrey told me that a good senator knew how to compromise on minor matters, but was willing to die, politically, for more serious ones. "The difficulty," he said, "is knowing which is which." Some ideas on the subject were also suggested by my reading. From my first days in the Senate I was deeply interested in its history as an institution. I read avidly everything about the Senate, from the popular works to the scholarly.

Among the books I studied was *The Public Philosophy,* by Walter Lippmann. This author saw the tendency to suppress viewpoints different from those of the majority as one of the great dangers to a democracy. And in that regard, he considered the Senate to be a special kind of safeguarding institution. "In the Senate of the United States, for example," he wrote, "a Senator can be promptly challenged by another Senator and brought to an accounting. Here among the Senators themselves the conditions are most nearly ideal for the toleration of all opinions."

Who does a public official represent? Lippmann wrote, and I agreed with him, that a public official represents *"The People"*—that is, "a community of the entire living population, with their predecessors and successors"—and not just "the voters." A good senator must be like a good lawyer, acting as his client's partisan and advocate, but still bound by law and ethics and his own good judgment and sense of right and wrong. Courage, then, is the courage to represent *"The People,"* while hoping to get re-elected by "the voters."

And that's a difficult enterprise. For, as Lippmann wrote, "the general rule is that a democratic politician had better not be right too soon. Very often the penalty is political death. It is much safer to keep in step with the parade of opinion than to try to keep up with the swifter movement of events."

The Senate reception room always fascinated me because it contained the painted portraits of five great former senators—Daniel Webster, John C. Calhoun, Henry Clay, Robert M. La Follette, Sr., and Robert A. Taft. I wondered how and why they had been chosen.

The Capitol, seat of the United States Congress, was built in stages. Once, it was only a square, sandstone-and-granite four-story box. Then there were two such buildings, connected by a wooden walkway. Later, these buildings were joined in stone. Still later, just prior to the Civil War, construction was begun on the massive, cast-iron dome in the middle, and new wings were added on each end. Today, sprawling astride Capitol Hill, overlooking downtown Washington and the White House to the west, the gleaming white building stretches from Constitution Avenue on the north to Independence Avenue on the south. The great white dome, lighted at night and crowned with a statue of Freedom, dominates the capital city and symbolizes American democracy.

The Capitol is under the exclusive jurisdiction of Congress. The middle of the dome is the dividing line between the territories of the two houses. To the north of that line, the Senate is supreme; to the south, the House of Representatives. Each house flies an American flag over its own wing during the hours when it is in session.

The Senate reception room is located in the northeast corner of the building, just off the Senate chamber. Here, when the Senate is in session, members meet with friends, constituents, and lobbyists. Three young aides, stationed at a small table, carry in messages to senators on the floor.

The room is large and rectangular, and almost entirely covered with one or another form of intricately ornate art work, completed by Constantino Brumidi, an Italian immigrant artist, in 1874. Geometric designs in tiles of light rust, cream yellow, and blue spread across the floor, culminating in the middle in a twelve-pointed star, slightly off center. Two massive crystal chandeliers, all glittering prisms and dazzling glass-bead ropes, light the room and cast reflections upward on the golds and blues and browns and painted cherubs and madonnas of the ceiling, half of which forms a dome, while the other is vaulted.

On the north wall, straight ahead as a visitor enters, are two gold-crowned, nine-foot windows. Beneath each window is a brown leather window seat for two, set back into the wall. Between the windows and above the mantle of a small marble fireplace, which no longer works, is a massive, gold-framed mirror, six feet tall. At that end of the room, too, is a long walnut conference table, surrounded by walnut chairs with brown leather seats and backs. All along the walls are uncomfortable high-backed walnut benches. On the west side of the room is the guarded door to the Senate lobby, which is closed to the public, as is the Senate chamber. There is a kind of forbidding and intimidating formality about the reception room which says to the visitor, You are an outsider here, and this is as far as you can go.

The walls of the room are covered with a brown and tan profusion of painted doves and cherubs and curlicues and geometric designs and a maze of raised, gold-leaf vines and fruit and leaves. High on the south wall is a painting of a meeting between Jefferson, Hamilton, and Washington—unique in that Jefferson is shown without a wig and with unpowdered hair, and his hair is red.

But the room is best known for its portraits of five outstanding former senators, painted directly on the walls in oval panels left vacant by Brumidi. Each panel is topped by a raised, gold-leaf eagle with lightning bolts and arrows in his claws, and is surrounded by raised, gold-leaf vines and leaves, intertwined in which are two golden snakes, one on each side of the portrait, their forked tongues darting forth. American Indians might make something of this symbolism.

To this room, at 12:30 P.M. on Thursday, March 12, 1959, came Vice-President Richard Nixon, Senator John F. Kennedy, Senator Lyndon Johnson, Senator Everett Dirksen, and a host of other important senators and guests, for the unveiling of the five portraits.

In 1964, as a new senator, I combed the stacks of the Library of Congress for information about how the subjects of these portraits had been chosen. I learned a little from old newspaper and magazine articles. But I found that even the official record of the proceedings at the unveiling was out of print and unavailable. Finally, Robert Kennedy had a search made of his late brother's papers and secured for me the unpublished private files on the selection. Since John F. Kennedy had been chairman of the selection committee, these files were a gold mine. They contained the written opinions of more than a hundred historians, and original letters from former presidents Harry S. Truman and Herbert Hoover and numerous senators of the time.

The selection committee was Senate Majority Leader Lyndon Johnson's idea. From his bed in Bethesda Naval Hospital, where he was convalescing from a heart attack, Johnson still dominated the Senate. In August, 1955, he caused a resolution to be introduced and adopted in the Senate to create a special committee on the Senate reception room to ". . . select five outstanding persons from among all persons, but not a living person, who have served as members of the Senate since the formation of the government of the United States, whose paintings shall be placed in the five unfilled spaces of the Senate Reception Room."

But the idea was not totally original with Johnson. Back in 1870, Senator Justin Morrill of Vermont had written to the Architect of the Capitol, suggesting that an artist be commissioned to paint portraits in the blank panels. In speaking of this earlier suggestion, Vice-President Nixon drew considerable laughter from the assembled crowd at the unveiling ceremony in 1959, eighty-nine years after Morrill's letter, when he said, "No action was taken. Or should I say that the Senate acted in its usual, very deliberate way?"

In any event, the Senate finally did get around to appointing a selection committee, and young John F. Kennedy of Massachusetts, who had just written *Profiles in Courage,* a collection of accounts of exceptional senatorial courage, awarded a Pulitzer Prize in 1957, was chosen as its chairman. In commenting on the appointments to the committee, *The Reporter* magazine observed that Kennedy was a natural choice for chairman. "Democratic conservatism is represented by Richard Russell of Georgia, and Western liberalism by Mike Mansfield of Montana," the magazine said; it then continued, with tongue in cheek, "Serving with them are men of such proven historical judgment as Styles Bridges of New Hampshire and John Bricker of Ohio."

As the selection committee began its work, *The Reporter* said, "It may well be that the most exciting controversy of an altogether dull session of Congress will come over the Senators' efforts to select the five greatest of their deceased predecessors." Indeed, it seemed that almost everyone had a favorite nominee, and mail began to pour in to the committee's office. Kennedy wrote an article for the *New York Times Magazine* in which he suggested that it might be necessary to compromise by building a *new* reception room, featuring forty-eight portraits.

From the first, the toughest problem of the selection committee was how to define "greatness" in a senator. Kennedy wrote that a test based on legislative accomplishment was very difficult to apply. Some senators are best remembered for their "courageous negation," not for what they accomplished, he said. Some senators failed in a legislative effort in their own time, but their advocacy eventually led others, perhaps years later, to take up the same cause and succeed. And, Kennedy wrote, the popular association of an individual with a major piece of legislation can sometimes be misleading. He cited John Sherman of Ohio as a case in point. Sherman is hailed as the author of the Sherman Silver Purchase Act and the landmark Sherman Antitrust Act, but—Kennedy pointed out—Sherman's close friend and fellow senator George Frisbie Hoar had once said that the silver bill had actually been adopted over Sherman's protest and that the antitrust bill had been introduced by request and with little personal interest. Hoar had added, concerning the latter bill, "I doubt very much whether he [Sherman] read it. If he did, I do not think he ever understood it."

Kennedy wrote, too, that length of service in the Senate was not a valid test, because it sometimes indicated nothing more than local political success.

"If personal integrity is the test," Kennedy continued, "we must exclude Daniel Webster who saw to it that his 'usual retainer' was 'refreshed' by the National Bank when its charter came up for Senate renewal. If national leadership is required, we must exclude John C. Calhoun who lived—and died—for Southern principles. If contemporary popularity is essential, we must exclude George Norris upon whose name (because of his filibuster against Wilson's armed-ship bill in 1917) The New York Times once editorialized 'the odium of treasonable purpose will rest forevermore.' . . .

"Finally, if we adopt the suggestion of many that we select those who were statesmen and *not* politicians, whom can we include? Not Clay, scheming for the Presidency; not Calhoun, embarrassing Jackson and conspiring against Benton; not Webster, earning Emerson's epitaph, 'A great man with a small ambition'; not Presidential candidates like Douglas or Taft or La Follette or Houston; not party spokesmen like Vandenberg or Benton. I know of no man elected to the Senate in all its history who was not a 'politician,' whether or not he was also a 'statesman.' "

The Reporter, too, pointed out the difficulties with the "greatness" test. "A little foresight should have made it obvious that such an enterprise was destined for trouble," the magazine said. "First, how to define 'greatness'? Is it simply the quality of courage that Kennedy wrote about so eloquently? But this courage was usually displayed in defying other Senators. In such cases, one Senator's courage is another Senator's pigheadedness."

Kennedy, and the selection committee as a whole, came to the conclusion that there were no standard tests that could be applied to all nominees equally. Kennedy wrote that "the value of a Senator is not so easily determined as the value of a car or a hog, or even that of a public utility bond or a ballplayer. There are no standard tests to apply to a Senator, no Dun & Bradstreet rating, no scouting reports." The committee even decided to stop calling its efforts a search for the five *greatest* senators, making a special point of the fact that in strict accordance with the definition of the task in Johnson's resolution, it would choose five *outstanding* senators—not even the five *most* outstanding.

The committee solicited the views, among others, of former presidents Harry S. Truman and Herbert Hoover. Truman responded, characteristically, with a richly annotated list of thirty-nine names and offered to discuss them personally with Kennedy and the committee. Hoover wrote that he did not feel that he had sufficient knowledge to make a choice. "I suppose Clay and Webster would be eligible for consideration," he said, adding also that "the Sherman Anti-Trust Law was one of the greatest preservatives of the American way of life."

A panel of historians chaired by Allan Nevins, a Columbia professor and twice winner of the Pulitzer Prize for biography, was appointed by the Senate committee to assist with the selection. The committee sent letters to 150 prominent scholars throughout the country, seeking nominations. The criteria stated in these letters were not very helpful: "First, that the Senators should be chosen without regard for their service in other offices; second, that they should be distinguished for acts of statesmanship transcending party and state lines; and third, that the definition of 'statesmanship' may well include leadership in national thought and Constitutional interpretation as well as in legislation."

When the scholars' ballots were counted, Clay, Webster, and George W. Norris of Nebraska led the field with eighty-four votes each. Calhoun was next with sixty-one, followed by La Follette with forty-four. The scholars ranked Stephen A. Douglas of Illinois, Arthur Vandenberg of Michigan and Thomas Hart Benton of Missouri sixth, seventh, and eighth. Robert Taft was ninth on the list, with twenty-two votes.

But in the end Taft was selected and Norris was not, primarily because of pressure from sitting senators. The senators of the day took considerable interest in the work of the selection committee. *Newsweek* reported that the committee's job had started out as a "simple problem in interior decoration"—how to fill the blank panels in the reception room—but that "Senators have fretted and fumed about it."

Too many senators, with an eye toward their home-state press, pushed for the selection of a native son. Senator Ralph Flanders of Vermont nominated Justin Morrill of Vermont, author of the bill establishing land-grant colleges—the same Morrill who had been the first, back in 1870, to suggest the reception-room portraits. Senator Sam Ervin, Jr., of North Carolina nominated Willie Person Mangum and Zebulon Vance of North Carolina, giving no reasons or arguments in support of his choices.

Senator Kerr of Oklahoma nominated Oklahoma's first United States senators, Robert L. Owen and Thomas P. Gore. I myself have always been intrigued by Gore, who came from my home town of Lawton. He started out as a Populist and wound up as a reactionary. He once lost his Senate seat because of his opposition to Wilson's League of Nations, regained it, and then lost it again because of his opposition to Roosevelt's New Deal. As Senator Kerr wrote to the Kennedy committee about Gore, "He was a man of high courage and determination, who once having taken a position rarely revised it, though an overwhelming public opinion demanded that he do so." Gore was totally blind, and he was crusty, tough, and plain-spoken. The late Senator Richard Russell, who served with Gore almost before I was born, once described to me a heated confrontation between Gore and another senator on the floor of the Senate. In those days, there were no microphones in the chamber, so when senators spoke to each other under their breath, their words could not be heard in the galleries. Senator Russell said that one time, in the midst of a bitter debate, the senator who was Gore's angry antagonist said under his breath, "If you weren't blind, I'd trash you within an inch of your life."

Without a moment's hesitation, Russell told me, Gore wheeled toward his challenger and said, "Blindfold the son of a bitch and point him in my direction!"

A number of senators gave serious thought to the selection of national figures. Jacob Javits of New York nominated Clay, La Follette, Norris, Webster, and Edmund Ross of Kansas. Estes Kefauver of Tennessee nominated Norris and Cordell Hull.

Senator Paul Douglas of Illinois objected to the choice of either Webster or Calhoun. "I should like to protest the possible inclusion of Daniel Webster," Douglas wrote Kennedy, "because while able and influential, he was undoubtedly venal—see Reginald C. McGrane, *The Correspondence of Nicholas Biddle Dealing with National Affairs,* 1807–1844 and S. F. Bemis' book on John Quincy Adams, and the diplomacy of the period. I would also reject John C. Calhoun because although he was a man of great intellect, he devoted his talents to the defense of slavery and inequality, principles hostile to the deepest faith of America." Douglas nominated Clay, Norris, La Follette, and Benton.

Kennedy was sufficiently concerned about Douglas's criticism of Webster to write directly to Professor Bemis at Yale, seeking reassurance. "Objection has been raised to the consideration of Daniel Webster on two grounds: first, the question of his acceptance of 'retainers' from Nicholas Biddle at the time of the bank controversy and, secondly, his acceptance of fees from Baring Brothers," Kennedy wrote. "In the second volume of your biography of John Quincy Adams you make a brief reference to this. Because these incidents may be brought up on the Senate floor I would like very much to get your judgment as to whether the acceptance by Webster of these fees should eliminate him from consideration by the Committee. In other words, is it your opinion that these were disguised bribes for which no legal services were rendered or that the legal services rendered were incompatible with his obligations as a Senator? There may be a differentiation between the two cases, and if there is I would appreciate any comments you might care to make on this point."

There is no record of Professor Bemis's response. We do know that in an earlier letter to the selection committee, he had himself included Webster among five nominees. And later, in the Senate, taking note of opposition arising from disapproval of Webster's financial dealings, Kennedy declared that "there is no serious evidence that his views would have been any different without these dubious connections." The objection to Webster was disallowed.

So was the objection to Calhoun because of his proslavery and sectionalist views. Kennedy was impressed by a letter from historian Arthur Schlesinger, Jr., who wrote of Calhoun, "He was wrong, but he was a greater man and Senator than many who have been right." And Kennedy said in the Senate, "In defending the views of his state and section on the practice of slavery, abhorrent to all of us today but a Constitutionally recognized practice in his time, Calhoun was yielding neither to the pressures of expediency or immorality—nor did his opponents at the time so regard it. Calhoun was not a proponent of disunion—though he warned at the end of his career that secession might be the South's only means of achieving justice, he fought long and hard to keep the South in the Union."

But the challenge to the selection of Norris of Nebraska was not so easily handled, because opposition to Norris was led by a fellow Nebraskan, conservative Republican Carl Curtis, a sitting senator at that time. As set forth in *The Reporter,* Curtis "let it be known that he thinks traditional Senatorial courtesy should be observed in letting a member have a veto over someone from his own state."

Norris had been ranked among the top three nominees in the vote by the nation's scholars. Clinton Rossiter, professor of government at Cornell University, called Norris "the model progressive." Historian Henry Steele Commager wrote the selection committee that Norris had distinguished himself "as a true independent in politics, as champion of the underprivileged in the twenties; as a ceaseless watchdog for the causes of liberalism and honesty in government." Norris had risked political death in opposing, as did La Follette, Woodrow Wilson's armed-ship bill. Kennedy was later to say that he himself had had great difficulty in excluding Norris in the final selection, calling him "one of the most courageous, dedicated men ever to sit in the Senate, and one whose influence on the public power, agricultural, labor and political aspects of this nation will long endure."

Whether or not the possibility of a sitting senator's veto played any part in the rejection of Norris, conservative opposition most certainly did. *Newsweek* reported, "When the name of the late Senator George Norris (Nebraska Republican, and one of the Senate's traditional great liberals) was mentioned, the conservatives raged; when it came to the name of the late Sen. Robert A. Taft, Ohio's great Republican conservative, the liberals raised an outcry." Eventually, the members of the selection committee worked out a kind of compromise. They had been able to agree almost at once on the "Great Triumvirate" of the nineteenth century—Webster, Clay, and Calhoun. Now they agreed on two twentieth-century senators—Taft, the conservative, who was the leading choice among sitting senators who put forward serious nominations; and La Follette, the liberal, who was a little more acceptable to the conservatives than Norris and who was not subject to a possible home-state veto.

The selections were made unanimously, and *Life* was given the exclusive story, which it ran with color portraits of the five senators chosen. Kennedy received a stiff reprimand from John Denson, editor of *Newsweek,* for granting *Life* this exclusivity, which, Denson said, was "so extraordinary in the conduct of public affairs." Kennedy apologized to Denson by letter. And in any event, the United Press broke the story ahead of everyone else, having received its information, Kennedy said, "from a source unknown to this office." As a result, it became necessary to hold the last selection committee "meeting" by telephone, so that the final report could be released at once to the rest of the press.

I came to the Senate five years after the portraits had been dedicated. They fascinated me. Clay with his piercing blue eyes and thin, stern face. Webster's proud, high forehead and dark, heavy eyebrows. Calhoun with his patrician nose and full, gray head of hair. Fighting Bob La Follette's defiant, challenging eyes and set jaw. Taft with his balding, banker look, his pursed lips and rimless glasses.

I studied Kennedy's files and speeches about the selections. I read the proceedings of the dedication ceremony. Lyndon Johnson had said that "character" was the common attribute of the five senators. Johnson had emphasized, too, that each of them had been a master of the Senate and that most of them had been thwarted in other, higher aspirations.

Everett Dirksen had called them crusaders and dedicated men, and he had said that they exemplified moral courage. I, too, decided that courage was their most important shared characteristic.

One thing was clear from my study of the five: none would have been an easy choice in his own day—especially not the members of the Great Triumvirate—Clay, Calhoun, and Webster. In fact, each of these three would probably have voted against the selection of the other two. As Kennedy pointed out at the dedication ceremony, Clay had once declared in debate that he would not own Calhoun as a slave, and had said that Calhoun was an ambitious fanatic and a selfish partisan who possessed "too much genius and too little common sense." Clay and Calhoun had often fought with Webster, and they had likely shared the view of John Quincy Adams that Webster was a man of gigantic intellect, envious temper, ravenous ambition, and rotten heart. And it was Calhoun who had called Clay a bad man, an impostor and a creator of wicked schemes, adding that Clay preferred "the specious to the solid, and the plausible to the true."

These were all men of hard, sharp edges. They made enemies, and they were unafraid of controversy. That was one lesson I learned from studying their lives. Another was that they were all human. I think we make a mistake in teaching our children a cherry-tree-myth, spurious kind of history which makes it next to impossible for them to imagine the Father of Our Country ever going to the toilet or taking out his wooden teeth at night. The role-model value of heroic lives is thereby diminished, cheapened. Clay, Calhoun, Webster, La Follette, and Taft were all human. But precisely therein lies their greatness.

Courage in a public official is the resolution to risk standing alone, if need be, before the firing squad of "the voters" in order to serve the perceived higher interests of *"The People."* The possibility of remembrance after death, actual or political, or the comfort of self-assurance in rectitude, or both, is preferred to the present satisfaction of contemporary approval and acclaim. This courage can arise from a lonely, dangerous, and messianic kind of urge, which some people live with daily, some now and then, and some only once. We rightly honor the public official who rushes into the blazing house of controversy to rescue what he perceives to be the trapped child of principle—even if the child later turns out to be a midget who set the fire. And the act of heroism is not made less praiseworthy by the fact that the official has on other occasions exhibited very human failings. Indeed, it is the humanness that makes the hero.

These *were* men of courage. Henry Clay had said, "If anyone desires to know the leading paramount object of my public life, the preservation of the Union will furnish him with the key." Clay was "the great compromiser," risking the wrath of both sides to forge three great compromises on the slavery issue in order, as Kennedy put it, "to save the Union until it grew strong enough to save itself."

Webster, the eloquent champion of "Liberty and Union, now and forever, one and inseparable," knowing that he would be crucified by his abolitionist supporters, had been largely responsible for the adoption of Clay's 1850 slavery compromise, which delayed secession and the Civil War for another decade.

Clay, as Kennedy said, was the most notable political thinker ever to sit in the Senate, and he was "the intellectual leader and logician of those defending the rights of a political minority against the dangers of an unchecked majority."

Taft was not afraid to go it alone, against his party and against the majority in the Senate, when he felt principle demanded it —opposing with equal and unavailing fervor, for example, President Truman's military draft of striking railroad workers, as unconstitutional, and the Nuremberg trial of Nazi war criminals, as being unjustified under international law.

La Follette, as Kennedy pointed out, was an isolationist in a time of internationalism, an independent in a time of conformity, and a "ceaseless battler for the underprivileged in an age of special privilege."

They were not always perfect; they were human. They were not always "right" by my lights; they were sometimes blind. But they were not afraid to stand up to adverse public opinion or to an opponent in the Senate. And at crucial times, they were able to say defiantly, with Thomas P. Gore, "Blindfold the son of a bitch and point him in my direction!"

5

All the Way with LBJ

The first thing that struck me when I met Lyndon Johnson was his ears. They were enormous, extending halfway up and down each side of his head. I was afraid, during that initial conversation, that I was looking at his ears too intently, that he would notice and be offended. He was a "long-ear," all right, like the imperial Inca rulers of the ancient Andes, whose ears were a mark of their royal status.

Like the Inca rulers, too, Lyndon Johnson was aware of every detail, even the smallest bit of daily news, concerning happenings in *his* domain. Hourly runners brought him reports from its farthest edges. He knew how road and bridge repairs were proceeding, what new reservoirs and irrigation terrace-works were required. His large ears heard almost immediately the scantest talk of dissension in his government and the minutest intimations of failings in his subordinates and associates.

I could muse along these half-whimsical lines during my first meeting with President Johnson—and not have him notice my looking at his ears—because I was not the real focus of his attention, although I was the reason for the meeting.

Sometime before, in the fall of 1963, I had been unsuccessful in an attempt to see Lyndon Johnson.

I was then only a Democratic *candidate* for the U.S. Senate, not yet even the *nominee* for that office. I was only one of the three Democratic candidates in Oklahoma, and the others, Edmondson and Gary, were better known.

President Kennedy was still alive at that time, and Lyndon Johnson was his vice-president. I was a relatively obscure state senator, not given much chance by national observers of even gaining the nomination, much less of being elected. I had come to Washington to learn more about national issues, and in the process, to make some news back home—to enhance my public image by seeing as many important Washington officials as possible.

So, I paid a call on the vice-president—but he wouldn't see me. He didn't want to get involved in a Democratic primary. I got no closer to him than the reception room of one of his three offices, this one in the New Senate Office Building. While messages were relayed back and forth—"The vice-president is in an important meeting, but I'll see if I can get in touch with him"—I looked around the reception room.

Lyndon Johnson was a Texan; that was clear from the paintings and other pictures: bluebonnets, longhorns, mesquites, cowboys, and windmills. He was also a politician. The usual plaques and awards and framed photos showing him with other notables indicated that.

And there was something else, too: a group of baby pictures arranged within a single large frame dominated the north wall of the reception room. There must have been photographs of twenty-five or thirty babies—some cherubic and smiling, some attractive only to their mothers; some with little curls on top of their round heads, and some as bald as Yul Brynner. What they had in common was that they had all been named Lyndon Joseph or Lynda Jane, or some other variation of the vice-president's name. They were his namesakes. Additional ones were clearly expected, because space had been left for more pictures.

I took my mind off my nervousness about even *possibly* seeing the vice-president by thinking about what my own namesakes' pictures would look like at that moment. It had been a standing joke between my wife and me that while a number of babies had already been named after her, the only creatures that carried my name were a dog in Bartlesville and a parrot in Norman. And the parrot had died, although being called "Fred" had had nothing to do with it.

After a time, I received word, that the vice-president could not work me into his busy schedule. So I left to see a soil and water conservation official, several members of the Oklahoma congressional delegation, and a GS-12 in the State Department. I held a brief press conference with Oklahoma reporters about my "fruitful" capital discussions and then went on back to Oklahoma to shake a few thousand more hands.

The world had changed when I finally did see Lyndon Johnson for the first time, in the late summer of 1964. President Kennedy had been killed, and Lyndon Johnson occupied the Oval Office of the White House. I was brought to be introduced to him by Oklahoma's senior U.S. senator, Mike Monroney. I was by then a nominee for Oklahoma's other Senate seat, chosen by the Democrats of Oklahoma to oppose Bud Wilkinson in the general election.

With the Atlantic City nominating convention behind him, President Johnson—along with the man he had chosen as his running mate, Senator Hubert H. Humphrey of Minnesota—was himself facing a general election campaign. But at the time of my first meeting with him, he was preoccupied with a legislative problem in which Senator Monroney figured centrally.

Mike and I came in through the west door of the White House. We waited for a while in a hall, and then in a small office adjacent to the president's office. A black-suited, elderly black orderly brought us coffee. His manner was properly deferential but still showed that he was quite aware of, and proud of, where he worked. The White House was a busy place. Aides came and went with papers in their hands. Telephones rang constantly and were answered in hushed but authoritative tones.

Finally, we were shown into the Oval Office, entering through a door in its west wall. President Johnson greeted us at the door. "How are you, Mike?" he said, with an air of burdened weariness.

The president's office was, indeed, oval. An off-white oval rug covered most of the floor; around the edges, tan composition tile was visible. At the south end of the office, to our right as we came in, was the president's desk, facing a massive marble fireplace, above which was a painting of Franklin D. Roosevelt, toward the end of his life, in a blue navy cape. In front of the fireplace, facing each other across a low coffee table, were two couches upholstered in an off-white fabric. Straight across from us as we entered, in the east wall, were three French doors leading out to the Rose Garden, their glass panes partially covered by translucent, off-white curtains. Flanking the fireplace were two doors painted the same pastel green as the walls; one led to the Cabinet Room, the other to the president's private rest room.

Directly behind the president's desk, in front of the concave bank of windows which looked out toward the south, were a number of flags, including the flag of the United States, the presidential flag, and an army battle flag festooned with a hundred varicolored battle streamers.

After he'd greeted Mike, the president turned to me, towering over me. He fixed me with the kind of disconcerting, searching, prolonged stare I'd experienced only twice before—once with the late Senator Kerr and once with Oral Roberts.

The president wore a blue worsted suit with an expensive matching tie. His pale-blue shirt had obviously been tailor-made. It had an extra-high, extra-large collar. The collar looked smooth and uncreased, as my own collars do only when the shirt is brand-new. The material of the president's suit was Brooks Brothers in its richness, but the cut of the suit was straight off the rack at Robert Hall's. The trouser legs were much too loose and floppy and much too long, lopping over his shoes.

After looking me over, the president extended his hand and said, "Fred, they tell me you've got what it takes, but you're in a hard race, aren't you?"

I tried to hold my gaze as long as he held his, but was unsuccessful. I said that, yes, I was in a hard campaign, but if *he* would help me, I thought I could win.

The president said that he would do what he could. "Old Bob Kerr would never forgive us if we let a Republican take his seat," he said. We were still standing just inside the door of the Oval Office. A White House aide and a photographer were hovering nearby.

"Let's take a picture," President Johnson said, and turned to move toward his desk. I followed. He sat down behind the desk, and a chair was placed next to him for me. I was seated on the president's right, so that my right profile and his left profile were toward the camera. As a matter of fact, I thought my left profile looked better in photographs, but when you take a picture with a president of the United States, he decides which profiles will be shown. At the time, I wondered whether our seating arrangement was purposeful or accidental. I learned later that President Johnson did nothing accidentally.

The photographer began to click away. President Johnson gazed past my eyes, his face turned a little more toward the camera than it would have been if he had looked right at me. His eyes were slightly glazed, and his face was posed as if he were listening to me intently.

I looked directly at him, rather than a little to his left toward the muffled wire-service teletypes and the three small television sets. And the camera caught us, much slimmer and sleeker than we were to become with the passing years.

The photographic session was quick, and the president soon arose from his chair, not waiting for a "That's it" from the photographer. He took me over to the French doors in the east wall and showed me, on the floor, the cleat marks President Eisenhower's golf shoes had left in the soft tile.

Then he motioned me and Senator Monroney toward the sofas, asking us to sit down. Mike took the west sofa, I the east. The president sat down in his Kennedy-replica, padded rocking chair, to the left of the sofa where I sat. A many-buttoned telephone was at his right hand on a low table.

Johnson proceeded at once to ignore me. Pulling his rocking chair up a little toward Mike, he went to work.

The president's first words came with almost explosive force, shocking in their intensity. "Mike," he said, "can't you get that goddamn bill out of the Commerce Committee?" (I've since forgotten what bill this was.)

Senator Monroney, who was and is a very gentle and dedicated man, visibly recoiled at the power of the attack. I was embarrassed for him as he began, hesitatingly, to respond. "There's some trouble with the chairman on that bill—" he started.

"I didn't ask you about the chairman," the president interrupted. "You're a member of the committee, and goddamnit, I want that bill out—now! Are you going to vote it out, or are you just going to fool around with little shitty points until the Senate adjourns *sine die?*"

To tell the truth, Mike admitted, he himself had some problems with the bill. The president countered, one by one, all the questions Mike raised, almost before Mike could raise them. The president's manner was rough and overbearing. I felt sorry for Mike, and I thought to myself that no U.S. senator should let anyone, even the president, talk to him like that.

Mike was courteous, and he remained cordial, but he held his ground. And abruptly, the president's manner changed. He leaned back in his chair, and his expression became more pleasant. "How's Mary Ellen?" he asked. Mary Ellen is Mike's wife. Mike said she was fine.

"Tell her Bird and I enjoyed being over at y'all's house," the president said, and stood up. An aide had come in to signal that other appointments or other business awaited his attention.

"Good luck to you, Fred," President Johnson said to me at the door. "You tell 'em down there that I'm gonna complete Bob Kerr's Arkansas River navigation project." Senator Monroney and I thanked him and left.

That fall, President Johnson came to Oklahoma to break ground for a reservoir which was part of the Arkansas River project, a multibillion dollar Corps of Engineers system of lakes, locks, and canals to bring freight barges all the way up to Tulsa.

This was an "official" rather than a "campaign" visit by the president, so neither at the ground-breaking ceremony in eastern

Oklahoma, nor at his later appearance the same day at the Oklahoma State Fair in Oklahoma City, was I allowed on the speakers' platform.

But both Bud Wilkinson and I were in attendance. Wilkinson and I, and our respective supporters, worked the sun-baked crowd at the dam dedication, and our campaign signs were much in evidence. Mine—like my bumper stickers—read, "Harris/LBJ." A couple of former Kerr staffers told me, only half jokingly, that the president probably wouldn't appreciate his name being listed last.

I had planned to hurry back to Oklahoma City separately by private plane, so as to work that crowd, too, when the president spoke there later. But at the last minute, although I wasn't on the manifest, a member of the staff of Carl Albert of Oklahoma, then the majority leader of the House of Representatives, pushed me on to the president's jet-powered helicopter along with the Oklahoma congressional delegation.

I was a little afraid the president would ask me to leave before take-off, and indeed he did not seem overly pleased by my presence; at that time the press was full of comment to the effect that Johnson was going to avoid getting involved in close congressional races, which might hinder his attainment of a huge majority over the Republican nominee, Senator Barry Goldwater of Arizona. Goldwater was in bad shape politically. He was being portrayed in Democratic television commercials as an irresponsible advocate of a super-hawk line on Vietnam and of the abolition of the entire Social Security system.

As the helicopter rotors began to turn more rapidly, the president sat down in the telephone-equipped command seat, his back to the pilots. I managed to get a seat just across the pull-up table from him. For a while, he talked with members of the Oklahoma congressional delegation about Senator Kerr's—and his—efforts to develop the water resources of the country. He addressed the legislators, whom he knew well, ignoring me.

But I was a good listener, and the president, like most of us, was drawn to a good listener. So, more and more, he began to speak to me, watching my face carefully for approval and response.

He reminisced about his close association with Senator Kerr, and he began to tell of Kerr's reaction at the Los Angeles convention in 1960 upon first learning that John Kennedy had offered Johnson the vice-presidential nomination.

"I had just talked with Jack Kennedy on the phone, and Bobby Kennedy had just left my room," the president said. I had avidly read every single report about this episode, particularly about Johnson's encounter with Robert Kennedy on that occasion, and I listened with consuming interest to the president's version.

"Old Bob Kerr came busting into my hotel room," the president said. "Sam Rayburn and I were talking, and Kerr charged in like a mad bull."

Then, President Johnson *became* Bob Kerr. Every Oklahoman knew Senator Kerr's voice and his mannerisms by heart—the imperious and studied way he looked at you with his piercing eyes, jerking off his glasses; the deliberate, oratorical way he talked, even in private conversations. And President Johnson before our eyes *became* Bob Kerr.

" 'Lyndon, I hope you're not thinking about running with that liberal Irish boy from Boston,' old Bob said to me." The president's voice, eyes, and facial expressions comprised an unnervingly accurate imitation of Senator Kerr. " 'If you *are,* Lyndon,' old Bob said, 'I feel like taking my thirty-thirty rifle and shooting you right between the eyes.' "

The president laughed, obviously relishing the remembered scene. Then, he said, Speaker Rayburn had asked Senator Kerr to step into an adjoining room with him.

President Johnson paused in his story and reached down beside his chair to pick up his white Stetson hat. He turned down the front of the brim, farmer style, and put it on. And he *became* Sam Rayburn, changing his voice and expression accordingly, as he continued: " 'Bob, you're in a campaign of your own down there in Oklahoma, aren't you?' the Speaker asked."

Now the president acted out *both* parts. His voice changed and became Bob Kerr's again: " 'Yes, I am,' Bob said."

Rayburn: "It could be a tough one, couldn't it?"

Kerr: "It could be."

Rayburn: "Could be tougher to run with Kennedy at the head of the ticket?"

Kerr: "It *will* be."

Rayburn: "Now, wouldn't it be better for you to have a neighbor like Lyndon on the ticket?"

The president took the hat off and laughed once more. "It wasn't long before old Bob came back into my room again," he said, resuming his role as Senator Kerr. "Old Bob said to me, 'Lyndon, if you *don't* take that vice-presidential nomination, I'm gonna take my thirty-thirty rifle and shoot you right between the eyes!' " We all joined in the president's laughter.

Newly mown Bermuda grass swirled up in great clouds under the flashing rotors as the helicopter set down in a grassy clearing at the Oklahoma City fairgrounds. The twin jet motors whined down, and the blades came to a stop as the door was opened. President Johnson put on his Stetson hat and was the first down the steps toward the greeting party. The day was bright and clear. A band was playing a spirited march, and countless thousands had gathered on the first day of the state fair to see the highly popular president.

A motorcade had been arranged for the short ride to the bunting-draped speakers' platform. The president got into the first car, the rest of us scrambling into the cars behind him. But when we were still a hundred yards away from the stand, the caravan came to a sudden halt, and we could see that, up ahead, the president had gotten out to walk the remaining distance and mingle with the crowd, "pressing the flesh."

I moved up near President Johnson as masses of people began to converge around him and reach out frantically to shake his hand. Some held up small children to see him. The Secret Service people struggled to clear a lane toward the platform, and the president began to move slowly along it, shaking hands with both hands, saying, over and over, "Good to see you. How are you? Thank you for coming." The great number of outstretched hands made a regular handshake and a firm clasp impossible. The president simply squeezed fingers, sometimes getting the tips of two or three hands at once in each of his massive hands. Frequently, a young person would squeal, "I touched him! I touched him!" Johnson moved methodically, professionally, down the lane of bodies, alternating his attention between one side and the other.

He was obviously buoyed up by this human contact. Those of us following along behind him were also caught by the excitement. The band music quickened our pulses. We smiled and nodded, pleased with ourselves, to those who occasionally called out to us from the crowd.

Suddenly, to the consternation of the Secret Service people, Johnson left the corridor which they had made for him and plunged through the crowd to his left, toward a line of saddle horses held by their proud riding-club owners. He stopped in front of a handsome but nervous palomino and shook hands with the cowboy-clad man holding the reins. "Pretty good horse, is he?" the president asked.

"A little skittish today, Mr. President," the man said. And without warning, Johnson took the reins, lifted his left foot to the stirrup, and swung up and into the saddle.

"God almighty!" a Secret Service man next to me muttered, "he's getting on the damn thing!" And, indeed, he was. The horse shied sideways a little, but the president gathered up the reins and got firm control of him. "Tall in the saddle," he galloped the horse off about thirty yards, and then wheeled and galloped back. The crowd went wild with cheers. The news photographers went even wilder, pushing and shoving and cussing each other in their efforts to get the best shots.

After that, the president didn't need to press the flesh to know that the crowd loved him. He moved briskly to the platform and stood for a long time, raising one waving hand to acknowledge the enthusiastic and sustained ovation.

The president's appearance at the state fair had been billed as nonpolitical, his speech being a "presidential address," and candidates were not allowed on the platform. I stood off to one side and listened attentively, squinting in the sun, as he launched into a major statement on Vietnam. To me, and to most of that Oklahoma crowd, Vietnam was a million miles away and of little consequence on that fall day in 1964. But we liked and cheered what the president said. He spoke as *President* Johnson, not as *candidate* Johnson. He seemed as assured and as in control of world events as he had been in handling the palomino horse a few minutes before.

Many people were demanding that he "go north" in Vietnam, the president said. He didn't mention his opponent, Senator Goldwater, but we all knew Goldwater's hawkish views. And the president made it clear that he was not going to yield to such demands. The crowd roared with approval when he said, "I'm not gonna send American boys to do what Asian boys ought to do for themselves."

After the speech, there was a VIP reception in a room under the grandstand. The press and the public were barred, but a friend of mine on the arrangements committee got me in. He also sneaked in Ross Cummings, my advertising man, and a two-member sound and camera crew. Ross wanted to get a filmed endorsement of my candidacy by President Johnson, for use in our television commercials.

It was amazing that we were not stopped. The Secret Service people were turning away numbers of would-be gate crashers at the heavily guarded door. Ross and I and the camera crew were among the earliest arrivals. As we entered, Representative Tom Steed of Oklahoma, who had mislaid his invitation, was engaged in a heated discussion with one of the guards at the door. Acting as if we belonged there, Ross and I ambled over toward one of the bars that had been set up at each end of the room.

In a little while, the president came in. He was very much at ease, chatting with various members of the elite Democratic group which had been invited, calling a number of them by name. Johnson greeted with special warmth three of Senator Kerr's sons. Somebody brought the president a scotch and soda, which he sipped as he continued to shake hands with well-wishers.

Before long, he had worked his way around the room to the place where I was standing with friends. He shook hands with me and the others. And Ross Cummings and his sound and camera crew moved in. The president knew as well as Ross and I did that the polls showed that in our state he was beating Barry Goldwater like a dusty rug, and he wanted to keep things that way. He turned icy as soon as he saw the camera. Ross held a microphone toward him, and Johnson looked down at it with the expression he might have used had the microphone been the outstretched palm of a Republican bill collector. With unconcealed anger, he looked around for a rescuing aide, but none was at hand. I could imagine someone catching hell, later on, in the privacy of Air Force One: "Goddamnit, I said no pictures with candidates!"

Ross Cummings, who has a lot of guts, moved the microphone closer. The camera began to whir. Other people moved aside, out of the picture, either through courtesy, to avoid ruining the shot, or—more likely, for those who knew Johnson—to get out of his range, just as people in a Western movie always scatter when the gunslingers start to square off. "Mr. President," Ross said in a reporter's voice, "would you say a few words about Fred Harris?"

Johnson was obviously seething, but he was also obviously conscious that the camera was already filming away. His face softened, and he turned to me and shook my hand again. Then he turned back and looked directly into the camera. "I need Fred Harris in Washington," he said, seeming to relish the performance, once he got started. "Send me Fred Harris, and together, we'll charge hell with a bucket of water. We'll tack the coonskin on the barn door, and old Fred'll bring home the bacon." Perfect, even with the mixed images! Ross immediately released the text of the president's remarks to the Oklahoma press, waiting outside. And that sound-on-film endorsement of my candidacy by the president soon became as familiar to Oklahoma television viewers as "Gunsmoke."

Johnson won by a landslide. I won narrowly. And I sat in the stands behind him on that cold day in January, 1965, when he took the oath of office in his own right and launched a new "hundred days" attack on ignorance, racism, bad health, and poverty—an attack such as had not been seen since the first hundred days of Franklin Roosevelt.

By Inauguration Day, LaDonna and I had already been

singled out for preference by the president's friends, from Jack Valenti to Perle Mesta. We were fresh and colorful—a young senator from Oklahoma and an Indian wife—and thirty-four years old. There were preinaugural parties and inaugural balls. There were small dances and even smaller dinners. We were in Washington. Lyndon Johnson liked us, and people knew it.

As I began my Senate term, Johnson didn't know quite what to say to me when we saw each other. At first, he fell back on talk about the old days with Senator Kerr. But before long, we began to get better acquainted. He was trying to remake America in the short time allotted to him, and I was a supporter of his program.

Johnson had come a long way from Texas, as I once heard Senator Russell of Georgia say disapprovingly. We were in the senators' *private* dining room in the Capitol, just off the senators' semiprivate dining room, where guests are allowed. The private dining room is so private that I honestly didn't know it existed for the first three months I was in the Senate. Actually, it consists of two small dining rooms, one for the Republicans and one for the Democrats. Each has a large dining table and a couple of smaller tables, and each has the ubiquitous chandelier and fireplace. Senators enter through an unmarked walnut door, which opens immediately into the Republican dining room. Democrats pass on through to the Democratic room in the back, nodding to senators at the Republican tables but not sitting down with them. In the back room, around noon on each day when the Senate is in session, Democratic senators, particularly the older members of the Senate and the Southerners, gather for lunch and conversation. The places at the ends of the long table are by custom reserved for the two most senior Democratic senators. When I first came there, Carl Hayden had the place at the west end of the table, his back to the redstone fireplace; Richard Russell had the place at the east end. Arriving senators, before taking one of or the other of these places, would always ask, "Has Senator Hayden had lunch yet?" or "Has Dick been in yet?" and only if they had, would others sit in their chairs.

I came in to lunch one day to find Senator Russell, Senator Herman Talmadge, also of Georgia, and Senator Lister Hill of

Alabama deep in conversation. Russell was expressing displeasure with the more liberal line Johnson had taken since he had become president. I joined them at the table.

"I told Lyndon in 1960 to look out for that A.D.A. and labor crowd," Russell was saying, "but he'd no more than got to the convention in Los Angeles before he'd thrown in with them."

"He found out where the buttah was," Talmadge said in the Georgia accent they both shared.

Kindly and courtly Lister Hill was having some fun with Russell. "But, like I said, Dick," he declared, "you can't complain now. That's your boy, Dick. You raised him, Dick. You made him what he is."

"Yes," Russell responded, shaking his head, "but as we say in Georgia, that boy riz above his raisin'."

Johnson and I understood each other because we talked the same language—not just figuratively, on issues, but literally. We could both jokingly use the same Southwestern expressions, such as "hunkering down like a heifer in a hailstorm," or "his eyes bugged out like a tromped-on frog," and we both resorted to a little strategic cussing when necessary to make a point. And we could laugh together.

The president once joked with me about the relationship between a member of Congress and a president. We were sitting in the small private room adjoining the more formal Oval Office, sipping diet cola. I was at the White House to urge him to take some action important to Oklahoma—to approve a public-works project, or something like that. Johnson was noncommittal. Ending the conversation, he got up and said, "Now, Fred, you go on back up there and tell your constituents that you really *told* the president." He laughed, and continued, "One time, a Texas delegation came back from a meeting with Franklin Roosevelt, and the leader of the delegation reported to Sam Rayburn that they had *told* the president this and *told* the president that. 'That's a damn lie,' the Speaker said. 'Nobody ever *told* Roosevelt anything; he does all the talking.'" I knew that this was pretty much the case with President Johnson, too—maybe with all presidents.

Senators aren't regarded as shrinking violets either. A friend who knew us both observed, "When Lyndon Johnson and Fred Harris are in the same room, there's one too many talkers."

Averell Harriman once told me that Lady Bird Johnson was the greatest first lady he had known, and he'd known all of them since the second Mrs. Woodrow Wilson. I believe Harriman was right. Lady Bird didn't come across well on television; her east Texas accent was a little too strong. Photographs didn't do her justice either. In person, though, she was a petite, attractive, very smartly dressed, highly intelligent, and warmly engaging woman. Harriman rated her above LaDonna's earlier idol, Eleanor Roosevelt, because, he said, Lady Bird had a much closer relationship with her husband. Lady Bird loved Lyndon Johnson, advised with him, put up with him, and helped to humanize him.

LaDonna and I had first met Lady Bird when she came to Oklahoma during the 1964 campaign, on the "Lady Bird Special" train trip through the South. We were both captivated by her. She knew exactly what she was doing, and she was terribly good at it. She was thoughtful and genuinely interested in each person she met.

It was at that time, too, that we first met Lady Bird's press officer, Liz Carpenter. In McAlester, Oklahoma, the main street had been blocked off, and thousands of cheering Oklahomans had come to see and hear the first lady. She was presented with a bouquet of red roses, and then Representative Carl Albert and I were to walk by her side, up onto the platform which had been built for the occasion. But as the three of us came abreast of an Indian group, dressed in blue and red and orange feathers and other colorful powwow regalia, Liz Carpenter recognized what's called a "photo opportunity" for the national press photographers, and she began to clear a space around Mrs. Johnson and the Indians, for a clean picture. Carl and I apparently didn't move fast enough, and Liz literally shoved us aside, saying to me and the majority leader of the U.S. House of Representatives, "I said get out of the way, goddamnit!" Liz knew what needed to be done, and she did it. I was shocked, but I've admired her ever since.

Soon after we came to Washington, President and Mrs. Johnson sort of picked me and LaDonna out from among the new people for special attention. In addition to attending regular White House social functions—receptions and formal dinners—we also dined frequently with the Johnsons in the family dining room on the second floor of the White House. We watched movies together in the White House basement, where the president always went to sleep fifteen minutes into the first reel. LaDonna and the president danced together at public and private social events, and he and I developed an easy, joking relationship. LaDonna and I paid no attention to the noise the president made when he ate, and we counted it a minor matter that, at the family table, he had his very own battery-operated pepper mill. In those early days, he was full of himself and pleased with his job. He was, anywhere, a commanding presence. His delightfully colorful conversation dominated any room. He was fun to be around.

Johnson was always asking me if I knew of any outstanding Oklahomans I could suggest for federal appointments. "It seems like the only recommendations I ever get around here are for Yale and Harvard boys," he complained. The first person I did recommend was Bill McCandless, the highly competent business manager who had headed my Senate campaign. I asked the president to name McCandless to chair the newly created Ozarks Regional Development Commission, with headquarters in Washington. Johnson seemed impressed with the recommendation, but he was also receiving other suggestions, and the appointment hung fire for some time. Just when the matter was coming to a head, I had to go to Germany for the NATO conference. I hated to leave before the appointment had been made, but Representative Ed Edmondson told me that the trip was really fortuitous. "Wait and call the president from Germany," Edmondson advised. "The effectiveness of a call to the president is in direct proportion to the distance from the White House."

It worked. In Wiesbaden, I asked the hotel telephone operator to get me the president of the United States, causing quite a stir. And President Johnson came on the line very quickly. He seemed concerned. "What's the matter, Fred?" he asked. I told him I was calling about McCandless. "Spell it," he said, and I did. He asked me to refresh his memory about the appointment and about my candidate's qualifications. When I'd finished, the president told me that he was satisfied and McCandless would get the post. That was all there was to it. The same process might have taken another month back in Washington.

Upon my return, I went to see the president. He confirmed the commitment he had made. And he went on to tell me that I had given him quite a start by calling from Germany. "Dean Rusk was here in the office when they told me you were calling," the president said. "I said, 'My God, Dean, get on the extension with me; old Fred's got over there and got in some kind of trouble.' " I couldn't help but laugh, imagining good and loyal "mine not to reason why" Dean Rusk, sitting there listening in and taking notes as I carefully spelled out "m-c-capital-c-a-n-d-l-e-s-s."

Time magazine once wrote that I was the only person in Washington who could have breakfast with Lyndon Johnson, lunch with Hubert Humphrey, and dinner with Robert Kennedy. It was true that LaDonna and I were personal friends of all three, and all three of them knew it.

But there was bad blood between Lyndon Johnson and Robert Kennedy, going back a long way, at least to the 1960 convention in Los Angeles. Johnson believed that Robert Kennedy had tried to block his nomination as John Kennedy's running mate. Robert Kennedy resented the adverse stories the Johnson people had circulated at that convention about John Kennedy's health. Each thought that the other had used money to secure convention delegate votes. And Johnson had, more lately, turned aside Robert Kennedy's desire to be his running mate in 1964.

Robert Kennedy never seriously chided me about my friendship with Johnson, although he and Ethel did *tease* me a little about it from time to time. Indeed, Kennedy once offered to support me for a leadership position in the Senate, precisely because I got along with Johnson and could therefore serve as a go-between with him. Johnson never said anything *directly* to me, either, about my friendship with Robert Kennedy, but he let me know he didn't like it. Once, when LaDonna and I were weekend guests of Robert and Ethel Kennedy at their home in Hyannis Port, the president called me. Ethel got up from the dinner table to answer the telephone. "It's President Johnson for you, Fred," she announced, giggling. "He's found you, and you're in big trouble now, kid." On the telephone, the president and I chatted amiably for a while, and that was that. He had wanted nothing in particular, except, I figured, to let me know he knew where I was.

Not long after that, Johnson found a way to give me the message a little more clearly. I was back in Oklahoma one weekend, when Dean A. McGee, president of the Kerr-McGee Oil Company, telephoned and said that he would like to see me, that he had something very important to tell me. McGee was a friend of President Johnson's, and had supported me for the Senate. I went over to his office. "I was with the president the other day, and he said something about you," McGee began, in a confidential tone. "I'm sure he meant for me to pass it on to you, or he wouldn't have said it to me. The president said he really liked you, but he could do a lot more for you if you weren't so close to those Kennedys." McGee then observed that I could do whatever I liked with the information; he had thought he owed it to me to pass it along for whatever it was worth. I thanked him and told him I would see the president personally about the matter.

The following Monday, I did go to see the president. We chatted for a while, and then the president said, "What's on your mind, Fred?"

"Dean McGee told me you thought I was too close to the Kennedys," I said. The president remained totally expressionless, making no acknowledgement or response at all. I continued, "Bob Kennedy is my close friend, and I'm his, as you know. And I'll tell you the same thing that I told Malvina Stephenson of the *Tulsa World*. She asked me, wasn't I getting too close to the Kennedys and didn't I know that they were trying to build a power base in the Senate? I said, 'So am I, Malvina.'"

The president smiled and changed the subject, and he never again, directly or indirectly, said anything to me about my friendship with Robert Kennedy. But he did later speak to me about my close collaboration with Mayor John Lindsay of New York on the work of the president's National Advisory Commission on Civil Disorders, the so-called Kerner Commission.

I had originated the idea of the Kerner Commission. Holding hearings in my Subcommittee on Government Research on the need for a system of national social accounting, I had become increasingly alarmed and despondent about the endemic racism and poverty in America. Little attention was being given to the terrible conditions in which most black people in the country lived. Then, in the tragic summer of 1967, the black sections of Newark, Detroit, and many other American cities exploded in terrible riots and fires. Much property was destroyed. Many people were killed —mostly blacks, a good number of them innocent bystanders. Passions were inflamed. Numerous whites believed that a massive black conspiracy was behind the riots. The black community was irate about the overreaction of law-enforcement personnel, and resentful of the unwillingness of officials to focus on the underlying causes of the disturbances. Nobody knew what would happen next.

On Tuesday morning, July 25, 1967, I introduced a quickly drawn resolution to establish a blue-ribbon commission on civil strife. With a few calls from the cloakroom, I had been able to secure the cosponsorship of Senators Mondale, Monroney, Joseph Tydings of Maryland, Quinton Burdick of North Dakota, and Ed Long of Missouri; and Mondale agreed to come to the Senate floor and join with me in speaking in support of the measure.

In my own speech, I cited the recent riots in Newark, Detroit, Cambridge (Maryland), and elsewhere, and urged that a commission, similar to the Warren Commission, be created. I said that I had just discussed the idea with Majority Leader Mansfield and he had endorsed it. "Actions which have been recommended by some," I continued, "involving prohibitions against interstate movement of persons who may agitate for riots, or which seek to find some common organized cause for such riots, however well-intentioned, in my judgment, do not go deep enough, nor do they recognize the national crisis nature of the situation."

The resolution stated, first, that riots and civil strife in American cities "constitute a domestic crisis which must be met and dealt with on an emergency basis." Second, the resolution declared that "lawlessness and violence cannot be tolerated or condoned in the American society, founded on law." Third, the resolution asserted that "equality of social, economic and political opportunity is the foundation of American society, and must be made real, immediately, for all American citizens." Finally, the resolution called for the formation of a commission, with members drawn from both Congress and the general public, to make urgent recommendations for the prevention of riots and the elimination of their causes.

While I was speaking on the Senate floor, it occurred to me that even before passage of the resolution by Congress, President Johnson could himself go ahead and set up the commission. And after conferring with Senator Mondale, I said in the Senate, "The senator from Minnesota and I will this afternoon dispatch a copy of the resolution to the president, urging him, as I now do, pending adoption of the resolution in Congress, to proceed at once by executive order to create this blue-ribbon commission and set it to its work."

The message and the copy of the resolution were sent to the president that afternoon. I called Douglas Cater, a White House aide, and asked him to see that they reached the president. I also asked Senator Mansfield to bring up the subject at a meeting of congressional leaders with the president which was scheduled for that night. The next day, I began three days of hearings on the resolution in my Subcommittee on Government Research. Professor Daniel Patrick Moynihan and National Urban League executive director Whitney Young testified, with heavy news coverage, in favor of the resolution.

The White House announced that the president would make a major television address on the evening of July 27, 1967. The word was that he would announce the creation of just such a commission as I had suggested. LaDonna and I had invited several of our friends over for dinner that night, and after dinner, we gathered in our living room to watch the president's broadcast.

About fifteen minutes before he was scheduled to come on, our daughter Laura, then only six, came running breathlessly into the living room to say that President Johnson wanted to talk with me on the telephone. I asked whether it was the president himself or a White House operator. Laura said, "It's President Johnson. He's right on the phone, and he said, 'Let me speak to your daddy.' " I left our excited guests to go into the kitchen and take the call from the wall telephone there.

"Yessir, Mr. President," I said.

"Fred, I'm gonna appoint that commission you've been talking about," he said. I told him I was glad to hear it, that I thought he was doing the right thing. "I hope you're gonna watch me on television," he continued, "because I'm gonna mention your name." I said that indeed I was, and that we had invited some friends over, too. "I'm gonna put you on the damn thing," he said.

"I appreciate that, Mr. President," I said. "I never expected it, but I'll do the best I can."

"Now, I don't want you to turn out like some of your colleagues. I appoint them to things, and they never show up."

"I don't know how good I'll be at it, but I'll be there and I'll work at it," I said.

"And, another thing."

"Yessir?"

"I want you to remember that you're a Johnson man."

"I'm your friend, Mr. President, and I won't forget it."

"If you do, Fred," the president said, "I'll take out my pocket-knife and cut your pecker off. You're from Oklahoma; you understand that kind of talk, don't you?"

I said I did, hung up, and went back to join our guests. "What did he say? What did he say?" they asked. I reported that he'd told me he was going to announce the creation of the commission and name me as a member of it. "What else did he say?" they asked. I said that, well, that was about all, except for a few private remarks which I did not feel at liberty to repeat.

That night, the president did indeed announce the formation of the National Advisory Commission on Civil Disorders. He appointed Governor Otto Kerner of Illinois chairman, and Mayor

John Lindsay of New York vice-chairman. Besides me, the other members of the commission included Representative James C. Corman of Los Angeles, a liberal Democrat; Representative William M. McCulloch of Ohio, a conservative Republican and civil libertarian; I. W. Abel, president of the United Steelworkers, Atlanta police chief Herbert Jenkins; businessman Charles "Tex" Thornton of Litton Industries; and Katherine G. Peden, a Kentucky radio station owner and political figure. Two blacks were also named—Senator Edward W. Brooke of Massachusetts and Roy Wilkins, executive director of the NAACP. President Johnson directed the commission to answer three questions: What happened? Why did it happen? What can be done to prevent it from happening again? "Let your search be free," he said. "As best you can, find the truth and express it in your report."

That's what we set out to do. We were sworn in a few days after the announcement at a ceremony in the White House Cabinet Room, in the presence of President Johnson and Vice-President Humphrey. We began to meet in the Executive Office Building, next to the White House. Washington lawyer David Ginsberg, who served as our executive director, put together a first-rate staff, and we all went to work.

The commission sent out investigating teams of staff members, authorized independent studies, interrogated government officials, and held extensive hearings. But first, we divided up into teams consisting of two or three commission members each and traveled the country personally, walking the streets where the riots had occurred and talking to the local people. Tall and handsome John Lindsay, urbane and sophisticated, was the nationally famous Republican mayor of America's largest city. I was a Democrat and had grown up in the little town of Walters, Oklahoma, where no blacks had been allowed to live. Nevertheless, there was an immediate rapport between us, and we traveled together. John and I shared the same sense of urgency about urban problems. We both felt deeply and cared deeply about the despair, frustration, and hostility which characterized black communities throughout the country. Our first trip together, to Cincinnati, was a searing experience for us both.

Shortly after returning from that trip, I went down to the White House with my Oklahoma colleague, Senator Monroney, to introduce to the president Jane Anne Jayroe, a fellow Oklahoman who had just been selected as Miss America for 1967. Johnson shook hands perfunctorily with Mike and Jane Anne when we came in. Then, when he turned to me, he said, "I'm surprised to see you up, Fred." There was a kind of mocking sarcasm in his voice.

"Sir?" I responded.

"I'm surprised to see you up," the president repeated. "I heard old John Lindsay had you down and had his foot on your neck."

I was too shocked to make any response, and the president turned and began to chat with Jane Anne. After the usual picture-taking session, Johnson took all three of us out to see his dogs in the kennel on the lawn south of his office. Then, having come back to the Oval Office, the president said good-by to Mike and Jane Anne, but asked me to stay on. After the others had taken their leave, he picked up from his desk a copy of that morning's *New York Times,* turned to a column-long story on an interior page, and said, "Now look at this shit, Fred. The *Times* says, 'Lindsay announces release of poverty funds,' and by God, you've got to read all the way down to the bottom of the damn page before you find out it's my program."

Before I could say anything, the president moved on to what seemed to be a different point, one about which he obviously felt very strongly. "We made a big mistake in the poverty program," he said. "We should have put everything through elected officials, instead of through these local committees that nobody ever elected to anything." That comment didn't seem to fit with his obvious annoyance with Lindsay and the *New York Times,* but he had apparently switched subjects and was just worrying aloud about mounting criticism of his antipoverty program.

"When I was head of the National Youth Administration in Texas," the president continued, "there was one county where the local officials wouldn't sponsor the program. So I came up here and saw Roosevelt and tried to get him to approve my idea of having the local Rotary Club be the sponsor for the NYA in that county. But Roosevelt wouldn't do it; he wanted local elected officials in charge. That's where I made my mistake on the poverty program. We should have put it under local elected officials. That way, when some jake-leg preacher went south with the money, there'd be somebody else to blame. Now, it's just me."

Then the president got back to the subject of the Kerner Commission: "Fred, have you seen the FBI reports on these riots?" I said I hadn't, but our investigators had seen them and the commission had interrogated FBI director J. Edgar Hoover. The president said I ought to see the reports myself. He called in Marvin Watson, his chief aide, and told Watson to get the FBI reports and show them to me the next morning.

"John Lindsay and I have just come back from Cincinnati, Mr. President," I said. "We both feel that this thing is much deeper than most people know, and that there's no conspiracy."

"Wait'll you see the FBI reports," the president said.

I searched for a way to make him understand better what we had found. I knew he admired Franklin Roosevelt. "It's just like in Roosevelt's time, Mr. President," I said. "Thirty percent of the people were unemployed then, and God knows what leaders and ideologies might have gained a following, if Roosevelt hadn't taken away their audience. That's the way it is now in the black sections of the cities, only worse. Unemployment is sometimes as high as 50 percent. We've lost the Stokely Carmichaels and the Rap Browns. They've been driven mad by the system, seeing people attacked and killed while trying to do the most system-oriented thing they could do—getting blacks registered to vote. But there are hundreds of Stokely Carmichaels and Rap Browns that you've never even heard of, and they are far more effective in their local communities. We may have already lost them, too, but we've got to think about their audience. We've got to respond to their legitimate complaints."

"Look at the FBI report," Johnson said.

The next morning, I did read the FBI reports in Marvin Watson's office. They tended to indicate that "outside agitators" helped cause the riots, and they amounted to the most sloppy mess of reporting I had ever seen, and I told Watson so. Lindsay and I continued to press ahead in the Kerner Commission meetings.

One or the other of us made virtually every motion that was adopted by the commission, and somehow, word of that fact got back to Johnson. That was the import of Johnson's sarcastic remark intimating that Lindsay had me in his power. One night, later on, following a dinner in the family dining room at the White House, as several of us senators sat down in the drawing room for cigars and brandy, the president opened the conversation by looking across the room at me and saying, "Fred, tell us about your friend Lindsay's campaign for president."

This time, I made fun of his concern. "Mr. President, you ought to quit worrying so damned much about Lindsay," I said, and laughed. "Hell, old John ain't got time to be running for president; he's already got more than he can say grace over, just trying to make New York City work."

In the meetings of the Kerner Commission, I kept quoting something I'd read of Lincoln's: "In times like the present, no man should utter anything for which he would not willingly be responsible through all time and in eternity." We decided, right away, that there were no short-range solutions. We also decided to tell the truth—first, about what had happened, and next, about why it had happened. In our answer to Johnson's first question, we indicated that there had been no conspiracy, and that there had been frequent cases of murderous overreaction by the police and the National Guard. As for the causes of those events in the summer of 1967, we concluded that most people in America, black and white, felt economically and politically powerless, and an overlay of racism on that sense of powerlessness had produced, for blacks, an intolerable and explosive situation. Once having decided upon truthful answers to those first two questions, we were already locked in to recommending deep and fundamental social, political, and economic changes to make things right and to prevent future upheavals: guaranteed jobs, a guaranteed minimum income for those unable to get jobs, fundamental reform of health, educaiton, and housing programs, and vigorous federal action to root out racism. Our report, running to nearly six hundred pages, was finally adopted unanimously after some tough fights within the commission. We planned to give extensive background briefings to the press prior to the time the report was to be released, on the day scheduled for its delivery to the president in a formal ceremony at the White House.

But one of the commission members, Charles "Tex" Thornton, who had fought the majority on almost every significant point in the report, got the false word to Johnson that it condoned and would tend to encourage riots, and that the commission had, in effect, severely criticized Johnson by finding that his programs were insufficient to meet the problems. Although I'm sure the president never read the report, the White House canceled the delivery ceremony. And someone, apparently hoping to lessen the report's impact, leaked a copy of the report summary to the *Washington Post*. When we couldn't talk the *Post* out of breaking the story prematurely, we had to release the full text to the rest of the press at once. With reporters scrambling to write whatever they could, as rapidly as they could, the published stories were, generally, superficial: "White Racism Is Riot Cause, Commission Says." At his next news conference, Johnson was critical of the report, even though, responding to Thornton's charge, we had sent Johnson a seven-page, double-spaced index of favorable references in it to his programs. All around the country, politicians reacted similarly, without having actually read the report. "We were poor when I was a kid, but we never rioted," was a typical comment. The only cabinet members who braved Johnson's wrath and said a kind word about the report were Secretary of Health, Education, and Welfare John Gardner and Secretary of Labor Willard Wirtz. The latter capsulized the report, in a favorable speech, when he observed, "What the commission has said can be summed up in the words of that great American philosopher Pogo: 'We have met the enemy, and he is us.' "

All the time that Johnson was president, I could tell by his manner, when I went through a White House reception line, how he regarded me at the moment. If he felt good toward me, he would hold up the line and continue to clasp my hand while chatting with me, never about much of importance. Society reporters would take note, as Johnson knew they would, and there would be plenty of time for news photographs of us together. When—from time to time—I was not in favor, Johnson's eyes would be hooded and expressionless. I would get a quick handshake and a weary "How are you, Fred?" and be moved on. I received that treatment frequently while I was working on the Kerner Commission report.

It was even worse when I teamed up with Robert Kennedy against a Social Security bill that the president wanted. The bill had a Johnson-sponsored increase in it for Social Security beneficiaries, but it also included amendments whose provisions were terribly repressive and punitive toward welfare mothers. Johnson opposed the welfare amendments, but he wanted Kennedy and me to let them pass and fight them later, in order to get his Social Security increase adopted. Kennedy and I refused to step aside, until we were, eventually, defeated by a piece of adept Senate maneuvering by Senator Russell Long of Louisiana. Johnson was deeply angered by my independence on that occasion.

And it was worse still when, very late in the day—not until the spring of 1968—I began to move away from Johnson's position on the Vietnam war. For too long, I had accepted at face value the White House briefings—full-dress presentations by the president himself, the chairman of the Joint Chiefs of Staff, the director of the Central Intelligence Agency, the secretary of state, and the secretary of defense.

My change of mind on the Vietnam war paralleled that of Clark Clifford, Johnson's secretary of defense. Before accepting that appointment, Clifford had supported the war. But once he had become officially responsible for its prosecution, he had begun to ask some fundamental questions about it, and the answers he received convinced him that the war was wrong.

At about the same time, after my duties on the Kerner Commission had ended, I was asking the same questions—and getting the same disturbing answers. I left the ranks of those supporting the war. Johnson did not take kindly to my defection—nor to Clifford's, as I later learned.

But at the last, on the Saturday before Richard Nixon's inauguration, I went down to the White House to see Johnson and bid him farewell. We talked for a leisurely hour or so, as, outside, boxes were being filled with files and personal effects and carted away. Once, we were interrupted by an aide who said that Secretary of the Interior Stewart Udall was outside and wanted to see the president about signing a paper to create a new national park. But Johnson would not see Udall. "Fred, everybody is wanting me to sign something at the last minute," the president told me. "They should have thought of it earlier. Hell, if I signed some of the things people have pushed at me, I'd go to the penitentiary. I'm just not gonna do it."

Johnson told me, then, that his main regret as president was that he had not been able to pick his own cabinet members at first. He envied Richard Nixon's freedom to do so. "But," he said in his characteristic, somewhat embarrassing style, "John Kennedy would have looked down from heaven and would never have forgiven me if I had turned his people out." Then he added a comment which I thought made more sense: "I had to keep his cabinet in order to maintain some continuity."

Johnson repeated that same thought to me when I visited him at his Texas ranch in April, 1969. I was by then chairperson of the Democratic National Committee. He agreed to see me only on condition that the meeting be kept secret; he did not want the press to write that he was trying to interfere in political or party affairs. We spent the whole day together, driving around the ranch in his yellow Lincoln convertible, with the top down, visiting his birthplace, touring his home, and just sitting around, having a cold beer and eating lunch. The president knew the history of each kind of deer that roamed his mesquite-grown acres. "Now, you see that deer there; that's one that Prince Sihanouk sent me from Cambodia," he would say. He had detailed knowledge about everything and everybody on the ranch. Once he stopped as we passed a young Chicano boy. "Manuel," the president said, "are you still trying to sell that pony?" The boy said he was. "What are you wantin' for him?" When the boy named a figure, the president said, "Too much." Later, we stopped at a grain drill being worked on by one of the ranch employees. "Are you going to have enough pasture mix to finish out the field?" Johnson asked the worker. The man said he didn't think so. "Finish the rest out with oats, then," Johnson said.

The president was proud of his Texas home, and he took me through it, acting as a tour guide. "Now this is Bird's bedroom," he said, as we entered a spacious, airy room with a king-sized bed. Lady Bird could be seen through the glass doors, out in the yard by the swimming pool, working on some papers or correspondence. Johnson picked up some loose pages from her bed. "Now, look at this," he said. I believe the date on the page he showed me was for some time in March, 1967. "Bird's working on her diary, and it says right here that she is looking forward to a year from this day, when we can announce we will leave the White House." Indeed, the entry did state something like that. I was aware that this was a big point with Johnson; he wanted it known that he had voluntarily left office—that he had not been driven out.

He took me into his bathroom. "Look at this mirror," he said. "Have you ever seen anything like that? It magnifies everything and makes it easy to shave." He made me try the mirror, and he was right. We went into his walk-in closet, where there was a long row of boots and shoes and a long rack of shirts and suits. Hanging on a stand in the corner were a large number of ties, already tied. "Now, let me show you something," Johnson said, picking up one of the ties and demonstrating as he talked, sliding the knot of the tie up and down. "When you take off your tie, just leave it tied, and it'll be ready the next time." I tried to joke with him, saying I was reminded of the way I had first gone off to college, taking two ties my dad had pre-tied for me because I didn't know how to make the knot. "Saves a lot of trouble and time," Johnson said, unimpressed with my humor. "But you've got to remember always to slip the knot back up after you take the tie off; otherwise, it'll leave a wrinkle."

The president told me that he had sold all the assets he didn't need and borrowed all the money he could borrow, because he was sure that Nixon was going to bring on a recession. "I know the bankers that backed him, and the first sign of the coming recession is gonna be high interest rates," Johnson said. He asked me not to quote him on this, because he hoped he would prove wrong, and he didn't want to cause a panic by anything he might say.

Johnson was hurt about Clark Clifford. Townsend Hoopes had just published a book in which he detailed how Clifford, a hawk before he had become Johnson's secretary of defense, had been the main force in causing the president's latter-day bombing halt in Vietnam, which got peace talks going. President Johnson felt constrained to deny that Clifford had played such a key role. I thought his protest too strong. "Clark Clifford and one or two others have been running to the *Washington Post,* leaking like a sieve, saying they were the ones that changed my mind on the war," Johnson said, and he obviously felt strongly, very strongly, about the subject. "Why, Clark Clifford didn't even know what I was going to say in that last television speech [the one in which Johnson announced a partial bombing halt and said that he would not run for re-election] until he heard me say it. Tom Johnson [an aide] and I were just going over the cabinet minutes today, working on my book, and it was Dean Rusk who made the motion for the bombing halt. Dean Rusk is the best man I ever had."

Nevertheless, somewhat inconsistently, the president later that day repeated to me what he had said on the Saturday before he went out of office—that he regretted most not having been able, at first, to name his own cabinet members. I thought that, ironically, in a reverse sort of way, Johnson was right. Had he been able to appoint Clifford earlier—his own man, speaking his own language —the Vietnam war might have ended sooner.

The day at the ranch had been wonderful, and flying back to Washington, I wrote a kind of sentimental, too-gushy note to Johnson on Braniff stationery. I said that I liked him, that I thought he had been a good president, and that I was sorry we had disagreed from time to time.

I didn't see him again until about a year before his death, when he came to Oklahoma to dedicate yet another reservoir that was part of Senator Kerr's Arkansas River navigation project. Lady Bird was with him. Both of them were relaxed, and seemed to enjoy themselves. At a small, private luncheon outdoors, LaDonna and I had a light and enjoyable conversation with them. Johnson's gray hair was long and wavy in the back. There was a built-in hearing aid in one earpiece of his glasses. "Luci has always been crazy about that dog, Yuki, and she's writing an article for *Ladies' Home Journal* about him," the president was telling LaDonna and me. "She's babied that dog since he was born. Why, she even supervised his castration, but they cut that out of the *Journal* article."

Lady Bird, who had been engaged in another conversation, caught only a few words of Johnson's remarks and interrupted to say, "Hon, they cut that out of the story."

Johnson replied, with an air of loving indulgence, "Bird, if you'd get you a hearing aid like me, you'd know that's what I just got through saying."

"LaDonna, I miss having you to watch movies with me," the president remarked, a little later.

"That's a damn lie," I said. "You never saw a whole movie in your life; you always go to sleep."

"Well, I still do that," the president said. "But Bird's gone a lot; she's been more places in America than Miz Roosevelt, and she don't have as long a step as Miz Roosevelt did. So, I found this little Catholic priest in Stonewall, and I get him to come out and watch movies with me. The other night, we were watching *The Graduate,* and, sure enough, I went to sleep. And I woke up just when that couple was cuttin' up. I punched this priest, and I said, 'Father, what do you think about that?' and he said, 'If they're doing that in Stonewall, I don't know about it.' "

I cried when Lyndon Johnson died. He had been wrong on the Vietnam war—but so had I during most of his term as president. There were a lot of rough edges in his make-up—some endearing, some fairly unattractive—but so it is with most of us. The main thing was that he grew to fill the office, and he showed genuine passion in his fight against racism, disease, ignorance, and poverty. He had, indeed, riz above his raisin'. And that's what made him great.

6

RFK: Ruth and Ruthless

I had not thought at first that I would like Robert Kennedy. For one thing, he was rich, while I had grown up in a populist Oklahoma family whose members were naturally wary of rich people. My callous-handed, sun-wrinkled grandmother Harris, with whom I had spent a good part of my early years—we called her "Ma"—had often said to us, in words from the Bible, "It is easier for a camel to go through the eye of a needle than for a rich man to enter into the kingdom of heaven." Ma had been raised in that old evangelical religion which taught, as one of her favorite hymns put it, "This world is not my home; I'm only passing through." She believed that, hard as her life was here on earth, if she could only meet the test and get through it, doing her duty to her husband, her eight children, her church, her neighbors, and everyone else, she would reap a rich reward in heaven. Those of us who grew up with that background took it as a kind of comforting article of faith, while we were kids at least, that rich people were *never* happy and seldom good.

This belief, I might say, caused some strange twists in our thinking in those days, because we were also taught that if we worked hard enough and lived right, the Lord would "prosper" us. And this second, conflicting line of thought was bolstered by the often-heard saying, "Money isn't everything, but it beats the hell out of whatever's in second place."

In any event, coming to the Senate in 1964 from Oklahoma, I found it hard to imagine identifying with Robert Kennedy, much less developing the kind of close personal relationship we soon came to have with each other.

Too, I started out with a certain antipathy for Robert Kennedy because he had once worked for the infamous Joseph McCarthy of Wisconsin, the red-baiting Senator whose irresponsible charges and threats had held whole segments of the country in paralyzing fear for far too long a time during the fifties. As a sophomore at the University of Oklahoma and campus president of the League of Young Democrats, I had publicly denounced McCarthy, thereby, incidentally, earning the first of many editorial attacks on me by E. K. Gaylord's right-wing *Daily Oklahoman*.

Moreover, there had been damaging stories in all the Oklahoma papers, early in the presidency of John F. Kennedy, about fully clothed guests being thrown into the swimming pool at Robert Kennedy's house, Hickory Hill, during a fashionable party, a party which had been attended by Oklahoma's U.S. senator, J. Howard Edmondson, the man I later defeated for the Democratic nomination for the U.S. Senate.

And in the election of 1964, Robert Kennedy had used the special advantage of his celebrity to defeat a good, progressive Republican senator from New York, Kenneth Keating, while I had been up against just such celebrity that same year in my successful campaign for the U.S. Senate against the famous football coach Bud Wilkinson.

But, happily, Robert Kennedy and I *did* become friends, despite those beginning impediments.

Our wives first brought us together. Ethel Kennedy was the eternal ingénue. At times she was attractively naïve, at times brilliantly and pointedly witty. A wonderful mother, cheerful in her duties but sometimes almost whimsically scatterbrained, she seemed like a cross between Mrs. Miniver and Mrs. Malaprop.

Ethel always said grace before a meal. She did it without embarrassment and with religious regularity and devotion, even though she was sometimes softly teased about the practice. LaDonna and I were present on one occasion when Ethel, as usual, asked all those around the table to bow their heads prior to dinner. Humorist Art Buchwald, who is Jewish, interrupted to say, "Ethel, why don't you ever call on *me* to say the prayer?"

I don't know to this day whether or not Ethel's response was serious; I have the feeling it could have been. "But what God do you pray to?" Ethel asked.

"Why, we pray to the same God you pray to," Art answered, without hesitation. "After all, you know, He was ours before He was yours."

Involved in important causes or the troubles of others, Ethel Kennedy could be as charming as Peter Pan. Defending those she loved, or her side of a tennis court, she could be as fierce as Captain Hook. Like Robert Kennedy, she was surprisingly shy with people she didn't know.

LaDonna and Ethel met at the Senate Ladies Club, which convenes in the capital each Tuesday so that its members can roll bandages, have lunch, and socialize. Yes, that's right: each Tuesday, wives of senators and former senators put on special blue-and-white-striped dresses and meet in a special room set aside for them in the Old Senate Office Building to roll bandages for local hospitals.

(The wife of the vice-president of the United States always presides over the "Senate Ladies." A few months after we came to Washington, LaDonna, Ethel Kennedy, and Joan Mondale, wife of Senator Walter F. Mondale of Minnesota, joined Muriel Humphrey, who then chaired the Senate Ladies Club, in a move to involve the group in more socially important endeavors—but to no avail.)

Each year's initial meeting of the Senate Ladies Club honors the first lady, the wife of the president of the United States, as well as the wives of cabinet members. Lady Bird Johnson was honored at the first meeting attended by Ethel and LaDonna. After they had been introduced to each other, Ethel immediately whispered to LaDonna, "Kid, stay with me; I hardly know any of these people." LaDonna is warm and outgoing, and I know that Ethel reached out to her because she sensed this. But LaDonna was surprised and impressed by such an honest and open expression of discomfort, especially from Ethel Kennedy, a well-known person whose husband had himself been a member of the cabinet. Instinctively and at once, LaDonna was drawn to Ethel Kennedy.

Not long after that first Ladies Club meeting, LaDonna accepted Ethel's invitation to lunch at Hickory Hill, which is two or three blocks from where we lived in McLean, Virginia. Ethel had apparently told her children about LaDonna being an American Indian, and Kerry Kennedy, then six or seven, stared at her in wonderment all during lunch. Finally, Kerry couldn't keep quiet any longer. "Mrs. Harris," she asked, "what's it like living in a tipi?"

LaDonna started, good-naturedly, to explain to Kerry that Indians no longer live in tipis, but Ethel interrupted. "Kid," she said, laughing, "don't disillusion her!"

LaDonna laughed too, and said, "But I don't want her to grow up in ignorance." And she told Kerry that modern Oklahoma Indians live and work pretty much like everyone else, except that they have the special advantage of their unique history and culture. Nevertheless, later, down by the pool, Kerry came up to LaDonna again and asked, "Can you shoot a bow and arrow?" The next time we saw Kerry, she was still fascinated by LaDonna's Indianness, and she timidly and touchingly presented LaDonna with a special crayon drawing, crowded with tipis, horses, and figures of feathered Indians.

Before long, LaDonna and I and Ethel and Robert began to see a great deal of each other. The Kennedys' social activities necessarily centered largely around their own home, with occasional small dinner parties in the homes of a few of their friends—people such as Art Buchwald, Rowland Evans, Charles Bartlett, Joseph Kraft, and their wives.

Through Robert and Ethel, LaDonna and I became aware for the first time of what a burden their kind of fame must be. They couldn't go out anywhere without being instantly besieged by autograph seekers and others. The frequent movies we saw with them had to be shown privately, at their home. Their residences—in McLean and in Hyannis Port—had to be virtual country clubs, equipped with facilities for all sorts of recreation and amusement, so that they could enjoy their leisure without having to face the public.

But it was great and heady fun to be with the Kennedys. Wherever they were, there too were "sparkly people," as Ethel called them. Receiving an invitation to the Kennedy house was as much a thrill for those who were great and famous as for those who were little known. To Robert and Ethel, the world's personalities were like the chocolates in a giant sampler box—a nougat here, a cream center there. And they were able to choose among them at will.

LaDonna and I never knew from one time to the next whom we would meet at the Kennedy house; the guests ranged from astronaut (later U.S. senator) John Glenn, to singer Andy Williams, to decathlon winner Rafer Johnson, to authors George Plimpton and Arthur Schlesinger, Jr.—or all of these might be there at once.

How did Robert Kennedy and I become such friends? His celebrity had something to do with it, I'm sure. LaDonna has always teasingly accused me of being about half star-struck.

Once, when I was in junior high school, my family was visiting relatives in Oklahoma City, and I went with two sisters and two cousins to tour the state capitol building. All of us were awed, particularly, by the gold-lettered door of the governor's office, and with unaccustomed boldness, we ventured to ask the receptionist if we could meet the governor. It happened, she told us, that the governor was out of town, but the lieutenant governor was temporarily occupying the office, and we were thrilled to be ushered in to shake hands with him. I still remember Lieutenant Governor James Berry's outstretched hand, his smile bigger than Jimmy Carter's and his shiny head as bald as a slick plum.

But, no, he would not give us his autograph unless we knew his name. We did not know it, and he sent us away, saying, "Come back when you find out what my name is." I remember so well that we stepped into an elevator, were asked where we wanted to go, and, perplexed, said we wanted to go anywhere necessary to find out the name of the lieutenant governor. Of course, the elevator operator himself knew the name—and told it to us. We rushed back to the governor's office, into Jim Berry's presence, and we soon walked back down that cavernous hallway, each triumphantly bearing a slip of paper inscribed, "James E. Berry, Lieutenant Governor." Somewhere, I still have that autograph, pasted in a scrapbook right next to a piece of cotton from the seat of an early-day buggy in the Oklahoma Historical Society Museum, a program for the "Ice Follies," and a picture of me and my friend Junior Hoodenpyle at the Fort Worth Fat Stock Show.

A part of being star-struck is the inclination to assign extrahuman qualities to the great and famous. As a young man, I wanted governors, for example, and other important people I met, to be perfect, and of course, I was inevitably and repeatedly disappointed. LaDonna never was. She *was,* of course, impressed at meeting important people, but she expected them to be no less human that anyone else. She expected—and accepted—their foibles, their imperfections, without making judgments. As time went on, I grew better at doing this, although I must say that I never quite achieved the equanimity she possessed about such matters.

Robert Kennedy, of course, was far from perfect, but he *was* about as impressive a person as I ever met. It is hard to think of him now without tears—ours, not his. About the only time anybody ever saw Robert himself cry was when he narrated the film about his dead brother, President John F. Kennedy, during the 1964 Democratic convention in Atlantic City. That night in that vast hall, we all saw him, vulnerable and alone, as he read the words from Shakespeare's *Romeo and Juliet*—words that were moving and yet, upon later reflection, somewhat bitter toward President Johnson:

> And, when he shall die,
> Take him and cut him out in little stars,
> And he will make the face of heaven so fine,
> That all the world will be in love with night,
> And pay no worship to the garish sun.

There were tears, all our tears, as we watched Robert Kennedy on television on the night of the assassination of Dr. Martin Luther King, Jr. LaDonna and I had been attending a Democratic fund-raising dinner in Washington, and the callous and insensitive chairperson had wanted, astonishingly, to continue despite the tragic news. But Vice-President Hubert Humphrey had acted to stop the dinner. Back home, we found our son, Byron, and our daughter Laura huddled tearfully together ·in Laura's room. We tried to comfort them as best we could. Together, we watched on television as Robert Kennedy, in Indianapolis, left off campaigning for the presidency and walked through the black section of the city, knowing that he could give the people there some comfort by his very presence and by the testimony of his own experience. On that night in Indianapolis, Robert Kennedy quoted the words of Aeschylus to the angry, grieving black crowd: "Even in our sleep, pain which cannot forget falls drop by drop upon the heart until in our own despair, against our will, comes wisdom through the awful grace of God."

"We can make an effort, as Martin Luther King did," he said also, "to understand and to comprehend, and to replace that violence with an effort to understand, with compassion and with love."

There were tears, too, ours and the nation's, as we sat beneath the high vaults of Saint Patrick's Cathedral, in New York City, and listened to Senator Edward Kennedy's brave eulogy: "My brother need not be idealized or enlarged in death beyond what he was in life. He should be remembered simply as a good and decent man who saw wrong and tried to right it, saw suffering and tried to heal it, saw war and tried to stop it."

Looking back, past the tears, to what he was in life, I find that Robert Kennedy is still hard to categorize. "Ruthless" was the word his enemies most often used to describe him. "Determined" or "intense" would have been just as good, probably better. And—many people will be surprised to hear—"shy" and "vulnerable" were applicable as well.

There is no doubt that Robert Kennedy was tough, but he was also enough of a romantic and sentimentalist to dedicate his first book, *The Enemy Within* (about his racket-busting experiences on the staff of the McClellan Committee), to Ethel, adding to the dedication, "See Ruth 1:15–18." In the Revised Standard Version of the Bible, that well-known passage reads in part: "Entreat me not to leave you or to return from following you; for where you go I will go, and where you lodge I will lodge; your people shall be my people, and your God my God."

I was drawn to Robert Kennedy most of all because of his earnestness and commitment. Kerry Kennedy was no more fascinated with Indians than was her father, and Robert spent a lot of time talking to LaDonna about that subject. But he was fascinated with *everything*. His curiosity about things, people, and issues was almost insatiable. When we first met, and as long as I knew him, he was—as I was also—learning, growing, becoming. And he was always questioning—whether he was speaking with LaDonna about Indians, with writer Jack Newfield about young people, with Jim Whitaker about climbing mountains, with Harold Hughes about the latest governors' conference, with Secretary of Defense Robert McNamara about the course of the Vietnam war.

Robert Kennedy learned a great deal from this relentless questioning, but it was partly a device, too. He was timid and reserved, and he didn't engage in chitchat very easily; the practice served to keep a conversation going without his having to say anything if he didn't feel like it. I'm sure many people went away from a meeting with him thinking they'd had a marvelous conversation, when actually *they*, under his prodding, had done all the talking.

Robert Kennedy was an unashamed moralist. He and I first worked closely together in some hearings on automobile safety which were chaired by Senator Abraham Ribicoff of Connecticut. Those were the hearings in which it came out for the first time that General Motors had hired a private investigating firm for what turned out to be an unsuccessful attempt to dig up dirt about our consultant, Ralph Nader, then little known. Our subcommittee was outraged. But, while I asked the General Motors witnesses careful questions, like those of a cross-examining lawyer, designed to uncover the specific sordid particulars about what the corporation had done, Robert Kennedy's practice was to confront the witnesses with the overall fact of General Motors' wrongdoing in the Nader case and force them publicly to admit their serious moral guilt. And by the time those hearings were over, the chairman of the board had come before our committee and publicly apologized for General Motors.

The same moral force went into Robert Kennedy's questioning when we worked together in hearings covering racial discrimination in the building-trades unions, although in that instance we weren't able to secure as clear an admission of culpability. And it was apparent too when, during hearings in California on the plight of migrant laborers there, a local sheriff admitted to a regular practice of locking up Chicano workers over weekends to keep them sober and out of trouble. "Sir," Kennedy asked the official in caustic anger, "have you never heard of the Constitution of the United States?"

Kennedy benefited from excellent staff work, of course, but he himself knew how to get to the heart of a matter. And I always had the feeling that when he became involved in an issue, he first made an almost instinctive emotional and moral commitment, and then put his staff people to work to come up with the necessary facts and reasoning to support the position he'd already taken.

Robert Kennedy may have been too moralistic at times, but there was no fakery about his attitude, just as there was no fakery about his religion. His Catholic devotion came from his mother, and it was real. He wasn't demonstrative about it, but its existence was understood by all those around him—made evident in ways ranging from the grace said at every meal to his regular attendance at Mass. Robert never spoke of religion in my presence, though we did sometimes discuss related issues, such as birth control and abortion, which caused him considerable inner conflict, pulling him between the teachings of his religion and his concern for women's civil rights.

And there was a kind of religious fervor to his commitment to causes, as I said when I spoke about him in the U.S. Senate after his death: "Senator Kennedy daily lived with enormous personal burdens of duty and moral commitment which caused him, with incomparable courage, to take upon himself the cloak of the alienated, the despised and the dispossessed and to become their voice."

In 1967, Robert Kennedy and I led the effort on the Senate floor to improve the Social Security bill which included highly punitive and regressive welfare amendments. We lined up other senators, parceled out among them our own sixteen proposed amendments to the bill, and organized our floor strategy and arguments carefully. Fifteen of the sixteen amendments were adopted.

But our victory was short-lived. A conference committee was appointed to reconcile the differences between the House and Senate versions of the bill. In those days, Senate conferees on a particular bill were automatically appointed from among the most senior members of the relevant committee—in this case, the Finance Committee—whether or not they had voted with the Senate majority. (That practice was later changed as a result of Senate adoption of one of the recommendations made by the Senate Democratic Reform Committee, which I chaired.) The Senate conferees on the bill, which Robert Kennedy and I had worked so hard on the Senate floor to make progressive, were all individuals who had bitterly opposed our amendments, and, in Senate parlance, though bound in principle to support the Senate position, they "dropped the Senate amendments as soon as they walked out the Senate door." The bill came back to the Senate in its worst possible form.

Most of our allies in the Senate felt we should give up the fight at this stage, because it appeared hopeless. It was December, 1967, and everyone was looking forward to adjournment. Also, the bill included a 7-percent increase in benefits for Social Security recipients, and senators did not want to see this increase delayed.

President Johnson was particularly determined that the Social Secretary increases should go into effect at once; so was Senate Majority Leader Mike Mansfield. The President sent three of his aides—Lawrence O'Brien, Joe Califano, and Douglas Cater—to meet with me in Senator Mansfield's office to argue, as did Senator Russell Long and others, that there was simply no way to get

Representative Wilbur Mills, then head of the House Ways and Means Committee, to back down from the House version of the bill.

Privately, Robert Kennedy said to me, "This is the time for some moxie." It was a word I'd not heard much. What he meant was, "We can probably bluff them down." It was late in the session. We had five or six shaky Senate supporters at best—and we weren't even sure whether they would really stay with us if we attempted a filibuster. But in the last days of any session of Congress, one senator alone can often get his way by being obstinate. And Robert Kennedy and I decided to be obstinate. I stood on the Senate floor and made a statement that signaled to the Senate leadership and to the White House that Robert and I were going to use extraordinary measures in an attempt to block passage of the conference report. "The pending bill presents such a crisis of conscience for all of us and such a moral matter for many of us," I said, "that we cannot stand and let it pass without being heard." This meant that we intended to be "heard" at length—that we would undertake a sort of mini-filibuster.

Mike Mansfield asked Robert and me to meet in his office with all the senators who would be seeking re-election in the coming year—including my colleague from Oklahoma, Mike Monroney. One by one, the senators said that Robert Kennedy and I were going to cause them very serious re-election problems if we delayed the Social Security increase by blocking passage of the bill which authorized it. Robert and I felt sorely put upon by this unusual procedure. Speaking for both of us, in as few words as possible, I simply pointed out that this was a matter of conscience for Robert and me and that we intended to do everything we could to block adoption of the conference report. I suggested that the majority leader and the other senators were putting pressure on the wrong people. I said that they should take the bill back to conference, drop the welfare provisions altogether—postponing consideration of them until the first of the year—and bring the bill back to the Senate simply as a measure for increasing Social Security.

The senators replied, in a virtual chorus, that nobody could make Wilbur Mills back down. "Then," I said, "he is the one who will have to take responsibility for delaying the increase in Social Security benefits." The Senate leaders promised that if Robert and I would allow the bill to pass, they would join with us and the White House in trying to eliminate its regressive features later on, during the next session. We said that was unacceptable. With what few troops we had, Robert Kennedy and I geared up for what the Senate politely calls "extended debate."

And we would have won, too, except for a bizarre lapse of attention by Senator Joseph Tydings of Maryland. In the closing days of a Senate session there is such a rush of legislation that nothing can really be done except by unanimous consent, so one determined senator can, by himself, gum up the works. That's what Robert Kennedy and I set out to do with the help of a few Senate supporters, including Tydings. The job of each member of our little band was to be present on the floor of the Senate and to object whenever necessary to the Senate's taking up the conference report on the bill. It was that simple. Joe Tydings was assigned the first day's floor duty. I went to the chamber that day just to make sure Joe was on the job—and he was, sitting in the back, reading his mail. Senator Mansfield came up to me while I was on the Senate floor and informed me that some senators intended to prevent the Senate from taking up any business *except* the conference report, to put more pressure on Robert and me to give in. He pointed out that if such a delay of pending legislation occurred, it would mean, among other things, that the appropriations bill for the Office of Economic Opportunity would not be passed in time to pay the salaries of that agency's employees. I told him that this made no difference to Robert and me, that we intended to hold out until the Social Security bill was sent back to conference and stripped of its repressive aspects. Privately, I felt that this news was so serious that it should be communicated at once to my principal collaborator. So I decided to call Robert Kennedy, who was in a committee meeting, from one of the telephones in the Senate lobby. Before leaving the floor, however, I took the precaution of reminding Joe Tydings that he was in charge and that he was not to allow the conference report to be taken up for consideration.

I had hardly gotten Robert Kennedy to the phone when Charles Ferris, of the Senate staff, rushed out from the floor, shouting, "They've passed it!"

"Passed what?" I asked, afraid I already knew the answer.

"They passed the conference report!"

"Where was Joe Tydings?" By now *I* was shouting.

"Sitting on his ass," was the response.

And indeed, that was unfortunately true. At the back of the chamber, Tydings had been going through his mail and messages while the majority whip, Senator Robert Byrd of West Virginia, took the Senate through its routine housekeeping procedures—approving the preceding day's *Journal,* adopting a motion to allow certain committees to meet during the Senate session, and disposing of other such mundane matters. Then, apparently, in the same dull and unexciting voice, and perhaps by previous arrangement with Senator Russell Long, Byrd had called up the conference report. There being no objection—Tydings was deep into his mail and took no notice—the conference report was *adopted* without objection. Worse than that, in a kind of parliamentary lock of finality, Long had rapidly moved to reconsider the report, Byrd had moved to lay that motion on the table, and the motion to table had been declared by the chair to have been adopted without objection. There was no way to reopen the proceedings except by unanimous consent.

I raced back to tell Robert Kennedy, who was holding the phone, what had happened. He was as incensed as I, and started immediately for the Senate. Senator Mansfield came to the Senate floor and delivered a very angry lecture, criticizing the tactics of Senators Byrd and Long. Joe Tydings took his medicine, publicly accepting responsibility for what had occurred, but that didn't change the result. Robert Kennedy delivered a bitter attack on Senator Long. Long responded, not without justification, I thought, that if you "live by the sword, you must be prepared to die by the sword." He said that if senators were going to take advantage of the parliamentary rules to block legislation supported by a majority of the Senate, they must also be prepared to have the rules used against them.

It was a bitter and unnecessary loss. But I was proud of my association with Robert Kennedy in this worthy fight. And I lived to see the day when most of the punitive provisions of that bill were finally stricken from the law—although we've not yet achieved fundamental reform of the American welfare system, which ought to be changed so that payments are made simply in the form of a negative federal income tax.

I have never forgotten how many sick jokes there were about John F. Kennedy, some of them persisting even after his assassination. But in some ways, I believe, the bitterness against Robert Kennedy was even worse. It got awfully tiresome hearing talk about the length of Robert's hair, for example, the criticism on this minor point masking a deeper kind of anger many people felt toward him. One reason for this anger was his stand on civil rights. Robert Kennedy, more than any other individual who had been in his brother's administration, was associated with efforts to move the country toward equal rights for black people. For example, he publicly praised the work of the Kerner Commission, which investigated the widespread riots which had occurred in black areas in the summer of 1967, when many politicians were scurrying to put as much distance as they could between themselves and the commission's finding that America was becoming two societies, "one black, one white, separate but unequal."

From the start, the commission had been under attack by both sides. Activists, black and white, charged that our report would be too conservative and would not really amount to anything. Conservatives said that the commission's members would prove to be apologists for black rioters and that our report would have the effect of encouraging violence.

Robert Kennedy was at first one of those who expected the report to be bland and inconsequential. He joined with Senator Abraham Ribicoff in a declaration on the floor of the Senate that what was needed in urban America was action, not more studies. And Robert privately thought that Mayor John Lindsay of New York was a lightweight and a dilettante. Sitting next to me in the Senate one day, Robert asked, "How do you like working with John

Lindsay?" The question was accompanied with a kind of laugh, and it was clear that his regard for Lindsay was not very high; this attitude had been bolstered, I'm sure, by the fact that Lindsay was something of a rival for public and press attention in New York. Kennedy was surprised when I answered that Lindsay was one of the most sensitive and hard-working members of the commission and that the two of us were collaborating closely to see that the report would be tough, factual, and fundamental.

But when the commission's findings were finally released, and received a generally unfavorable reception from the president and from politicians around the country, it was Robert Kennedy who joined Senator Joseph Clark of Pennsylvania in calling public hearings in the Senate to receive the report and to hear our explanations of it. Attendance at the hearings was so great that they had to be moved to the large auditorium in the New Senate Office Building. And although these hearings were held at a time when it was understood that Robert Kennedy was on the verge of announcing himself as a candidate for the presidency, he spoke out strongly in favor of the report.

Robert Kennedy became the central symbol of America's agony over the Vietnam war. I presume that as a member of his brother's cabinet, he had supported our initial intervention in Southeast Asia. And it was quite a while after Lyndon Johnson became president—and a while after I had become acquainted with Robert Kennedy—before he spoke out against the American war policy in Vietnam. I know that he agonized over this question, just as the country did later.

During the last half of 1967 and the early part of 1968, I was so engrossed in urban and racial problems and the work of the Kerner Commission that, frankly, I didn't give the kind of attention I should have to America's immoral and impractical involvement in Southeast Asia. When I spoke at all on the subject, I employed almost reflexively the hawkish phrases popular in Oklahoma, repeating the arguments I heard so often in the briefings by McNamara, Rusk, and Johnson.

Robert Kennedy called one weekend afternoon to ask LaDonna

and me to come over to his house to give him our opinion of a speech he was planning to make, for the first time breaking with the Johnson administration on the subject of Vietnam. The four of us—Robert, Ethel, LaDonna, and me—gathered in the small sitting room at Hickory Hill. The speech was beautifully written, passionately argued. Robert asked us about his principal worry at the time: whether it would be charged that he was breaking with the Johnson war policy for political reasons. Both LaDonna and I believed that he should not be deterred by any such concern. He obviously felt very deeply that the war had to be "de-escalated."

A while later, at a time when Premier Kosygin of the Soviet Union was visiting Prime Minister Harold Wilson in London, Robert Kennedy aked me to see if I could get President Johnson to make some private overture to Kosygin toward settlement of the Vietnam war. Soon after this conversation, LaDonna and I were at an intimate family dinner with the Johnsons at the White House. As the president was showing me and a couple of other people through the so-called Queen's Bedroom, I mentioned that I had "heard" that a peace overture, such as an offer of a bombing halt, delivered through Prime Minister Wilson to Premier Kosygin while the latter was in London, might be well received. President Johnson reacted quickly and negatively. He said that a cable containing a message to that effect had just come from Prime Minister Wilson, but that he had rejected the suggestion. The president added, rather sarcastically, that if Prime Minister Wilson himself had some troops on the ground in South Vietnam he might be a good deal less willing to take away their air cover by proposing a bombing halt. That was that.

With the completion of the Kerner Commission report in March, 1968, I began to turn my attention—much too late, as I later came to feel—to what was happening in the Vietnam war. Robert Kennedy got me and a few others together for lunch one day with Roger Hilsman, a former State Department official, who had just returned from a visit to South Vietnam and from talks in Paris with representatives of the North Vietnamese. Hilsman argued that the massive bombing in Vietnam was not working, and as a matter of fact, was probably serving to solidify North Vietnamese resistance, as well as world opinion, against the United

States. I found his arguments highly persuasive—and I began to change my mind about the war.

And the war, increasingly, began to cause terrible inner conflicts for Robert Kennedy. On the one hand, practical politician that he was, he had more than once endorsed the seemingly inevitable re-election of Lyndon Johnson and Hubert Humphrey. On the other hand, his criticism of Johnson's war policy was becoming more and more bitter. I remember seeing along about this time a televised report of an appearance by Robert Kennedy before the U.S. Chamber of Commerce. He spoke in the most outraged moral tones against the Vietnam war, and yet, when asked what he intended to do about ending the war besides continuing to make speeches, he was at a loss for a satisfactory answer. Something had to give.

As it turned out, although we didn't know it at the time, LaDonna and I were at Robert Kennedy's house on the very evening he decided to become a candidate for president. I had then already signed on as head of a national organization of rural and small-town supporters of the Johnson-Humphrey ticket, having agreed to do so mainly because of my feelings toward Humphrey. He was a close personal friend; we shared deep convictions about social, economic, and civil-rights issues; he was a supporter of the Kerner Commission report.

On the night in question, in the spring of 1968, Robert and Ethel asked LaDonna and me to come over and help liven up an obligatory dinner that they sponsored each year for upstate, mostly conservative New York newspaper editors.

I remember that Robert Kennedy was in a particularly whimsical mood. That night was the very first time, for example, that I ever heard him laugh when referring to his brother John. Standing to make a brief toast, Robert took note of the fact that President Kennedy's dark-blue president's flag stood near his chair. "There is no significance in the fact that the president's flag is so openly on display here," Robert said, his eyes twinkling, alluding to rumors of his own impending announcement.

There had already been a great deal of speculation in the press that Robert Kennedy was inching closer and closer to becoming a presidential candidate. Once, earlier, the subject had come up when a group of us were weekending together in Hyannis Port. Aboard Joseph Kennedy's cruiser, the *Honey Fitz,* we were idling in the bay. Robert and I were sitting off by ourselves, talking about the New York political situation, while Ethel, LaDonna, and others, including some newspaper people, were engaged in a separate conversation that somehow turned to the possibility of Robert's running against President Johnson. Suddenly Ethel called out, "Bobby, tell them how difficult it is for a person to challenge a president of his own party!"

Everyone became breathlessly quiet, and the press people, particularly, strained to hear what they thought might be Robert's momentous answer. "Oh, you must be referring to General McClellan's challenge to Lincoln," he responded immediately—getting off stage in a burst of laughter, without really having to answer. Robert Kennedy often used humor in that way.

As the dinner for the New York State editors drew to a close, LaDonna and I said our good-bys all around. Ethel and Robert followed us out to the hall. Jim Whitaker, the mountain climber, was also there, leaving. Teasingly, pointedly, Ethel said to Whitaker, "Jim, Fred here, you know, is Lyndon Johnson's campaign manager." We all laughed.

I took the occasion then, quickly, to say a serious word to Robert. I had seen his senior staff people gathering in another room for a meeting which obviously was to follow the social occasion. Now, as I shook hands with him, I said solemnly, "You know I can't be of any help to you in your decision, but do what your *heart* tells you, and that will be the *right* thing." That was the last time I saw Robert Kennedy alive.

LaDonna and I talked about it on the way home. I knew—and so did she—that Kennedy could not support Lyndon Johnson's re-election, but both of us doubted that he would actually become a candidate himself. We knew he didn't like Senator Eugene McCarthy, but we thought that nevertheless he would probably endorse McCarthy, as a kind of halfway solution to his dilemma.

But he decided to go all the way.

I never imagined that Lyndon Johnson would decide against seeking re-election. I did know that his campaign was in a lot of trouble. Senator Mondale had told me that on a visit to Wisconsin he had found the campaign there "going through the cellar." On the evening Johnson made his withdrawal statement, I was in New Orleans for a speech at Loyola University, and just prior to the president's scheduled television address, I was asked whether I thought he would really run again. I said that there was no more likelihood that he would withdraw than there was that he would suddenly drop dead; either event was possible, but highly unlikely. A few minutes later, I was interrupted by a messenger with a copy of the wire-service report that Johnson had, indeed, announced that he would not under any circumstances be a candidate for re-election. My reputation in New Orleans as a wise prognosticator suffered some.

Senator Mondale's situation that night was even funnier. He had agreed to watch Johnson deliver his speech—which was expected to be on Vietnam alone—from the NBC television studios in Washington, and to make some comments about it on the air immediately afterward. Mondale had prepared by securing an advance text of the speech, and had discussed it with some of the White House staff. He had been told that the president would add a peroration, but nothing to change the substance. So Mondale sat there in the studio, all primed to deliver his carefully prepared, though seemingly spontaneous, judgments about the president's new Vietnam pronouncements. Then, like everyone else, he was shocked almost speechless by the withdrawal statement. The difference, though, between Mondale and other viewers that night was that he was speechless in front of the cameras.

In New Orleans, following my own Loyola address, I went with some students and faculty members to the home of a priest, where we all talked at some length about what the Johnson action meant. Not until the next morning did it really dawn on me that I would now be on the spot more than ever. Once or twice since coming to Washington, LaDonna and I had discussed casually the possibility, which seemed fairly remote, that at some time in the future—1972 or later—Robert Kennedy and Hubert Humphrey might oppose each other as candidates for president, so that we would be forced to choose between two good friends. Now, the choice would have to be made in 1968.

When my plane stopped over in Atlanta, I called LaDonna and had her organize a meeting of some of our closest friends and staff members, and upon my return to the capital, I went immediately to this meeting. I wanted advice about what I should do.

Earlier, *Newsweek* had carried an item in its "Periscope" section, stating that if Robert Kennedy was nominated for president, I would be his first choice for the vice-presidential nomination; and I knew from *Newsweek* correspondent Sam Shaeffer that the source for that item was Kennedy's own press secretary, Frank Mankiewicz. But with the exception of one person, everyone at the meeting in my office agreed that I must support Humphrey, because he had the best chance of winning and of actually pushing through Congress the kind of social, economic, and human-rights programs and actions that we all felt were so desperately needed. We all believed this meant I would be forgoing the chance to be the vice-presidential nominee, since Humphrey was not likely to choose a close friend from within his own camp, a Westerner and Protestant like himself.

Typically, Lyndon Johnson had made his withdrawal announcement, which was of such enormous moment for Humphrey, while the vice-president was on an official trip to Mexico City, and had given Humphrey no advance notice. As the meeting of my friends and staff people broke up, I told them that at the very least I would not make a decision until I could talk with Humphrey.

Then, I moved to return a telephone call which had come to me from Robert Kennedy while I was in the air between New Orleans and Washington. Kennedy was no longer at the New York number he'd left, and I was given a number in Philadelphia. He was not available there either, so I called his Washington secretary, Angie Novello, and told her of my efforts to reach him. Vick French, of my staff, called Kennedy staffer Peter Edelman and left word with him also of my attempts to return the call. But Robert Kennedy never called back—and I think this was because we were too close. I think he didn't have the heart to ask me personally for my support, putting me, and himself, that much on the spot.

Humphrey returned from Mexico later that day. The next morning, at his invitation, LaDonna and I met alone with him and Muriel for breakfast at their apartment in southwest Washington. I counseled caution. "Don't let people stampede you into anything," I told him. "Find out, first, how much they'll back up what they say with public support, work, and money."

Later, when he decided to run, I became a public supporter of Humphrey's. I believe that even if Robert Kennedy had lived, Humphrey would have been nominated—and that in those circumstances he would probably have been elected. Robert Kennedy was growing and developing, becoming better able to be president every day of his campaign, but the polls showed him losing public favor in the process. The polls indicated that many people were put off—even frightened—by the frenzied crowds that mobbed Kennedy everywhere he went. And although Humphrey was avoiding the primaries—partly because he had started the campaign too late, and partly because of a bad decision—he was ahead in the polls from the first, and his lead kept growing, up until Robert Kennedy's death. From that moment on, however, Humphrey's standing in the polls plummeted. It seemed as if everything that had been said against him up to that date had been set in concrete.

LaDonna and I were plunged into despair by Robert Kennedy's death. So was Humphrey; so was the nation. The Humphrey campaign never recovered. I believe that had Robert Kennedy lived, but himself lost the nomination, he would have stood up with Humphrey and endorsed him at the 1968 convention. With his close ties to both Mayor Richard Daley and the peace activists, he might, I believe, have helped to quell the police violence and calm the street demonstrations. And being a practical politician, Kennedy would, I believe, thereafter have helped to legitimize the Humphrey-Muskie campaign. But none of this was to be.

When I first became acquainted with Robert Kennedy, I found his vulnerability, his lack of social armor-plating, both surprising and attractive. He was a highly private person. For example, he didn't like being touched. One day, he and I were standing together in the Senate when Birch Bayh came up to us. "What do you say, Big Bob?" Senator Bayh said, tapping Robert on the chin with his fist, locker-room fashion. Turning to me Senator Bayh said, "How's it going Fred R.?" and punched me on the arm.

When Bayh had walked away to greet other senators in a similar manner, Robert said to me, quite seriously, "Can you stand that?"

"I hate it," I replied.

"So do I," Robert said. Standing there, we looked across the chamber to where Russell Long of Louisiana was almost hugging another senator as he whispered in his ear; they stood so close together that their cheeks were actually touching. "If Russell Long did me that way, I'd say yes to anything he asked, just to get away," Robert said.

I was not particularly attracted to Robert Kennedy's competitiveness. There was something too fierce about it. This was especially apparent when he participated in sports. I believe that sports—football, tennis, sailing, softball—provided Kennedy a way to satisfy his need to have people around him without having to make conversation with them when he didn't feel like it. He was never so intense in competition that he couldn't laugh about it, but he was never so carried away with laughter that he relaxed his will to win.

Once, when LaDonna and I were with the Kennedys in Hyannis Port, she and I and columnist Mary McGrory refused even to try to water ski. "The only way to get along with the Kennedys is to admit in advance that you're an underachiever," Mary said good-naturedly—and correctly. Sometimes, LaDonna and I simply preferred to read a good book, or to talk to each other, rather than to get involved in some strenuous athletic activity. And that was all right—or at least accepted by the Kennedys—so long as we made our position clear from the first, and firmly. But the Kennedy competitiveness was very real.

One afternoon in Hyannis Port, we divided up, adults and kids, into two softball teams. I was the captain of one team, Robert of the other. He and I also served as the pitchers for our respective teams. Right up until the last inning, each of us slackpitched slow balls to the little kids like Kerry. But in the last half of the ninth, with the score tied, two people on base, and two out, Kerry Kennedy stepped up to bat for our team, and Robert pitched three sizzling fast balls in rapid succession—and *struck her out*. The game ended in a tie. That night, LaDonna and I and Ethel and Robert were joined for dinner at Robert's house by Rose Kennedy and Jacqueline Kennedy. And over dessert, I jokingly told Mrs. Kennedy how "ruthless" Robert had been in striking out his own daughter. Mrs. Kennedy remonstrated with him in a similar teasing vein.

"Can I help it if Kerry is a sucker for a high, inside fast ball?" he said with mock innocence.

But Robert was capable of tempering his competitiveness with the understanding of friendship. The first time I sailed with his brother, Senator Edward Kennedy of Massachusetts, I knew right away that I would never be as close to him as I was to Robert. LaDonna and I were staying that weekend with Robert and Ethel, and Senator Birch Bayh and his wife, Marvella, were staying with Ted and Joan. But when we split up one afternoon for an impromptu boat race—Robert against Ted in their identical sailing yachts—I somehow wound up as a member of Ted's crew.

I told Ted in advance that I knew nothing whatever about sailing. True—I laughed—I had been a member of the Walters, Oklahoma, Sea Scouts when I was in junior high school, but the only vessel we had been piped aboard in those days, at each Tuesday-night meeting, was a fake one, laid out in outline on the floor of the American Legion hall located over Calhoun's Grocery. I should have noted right then that Ted Kennedy didn't laugh at any of this.

It was a calm, hot summer afternoon in Hyannis Port, virtually windless, and the bay was prairie smooth. On a signal, our two boats set sail, Robert the captain of one, Ted, of the other, each working feverishly to catch every stray breath of the laggardly breeze. The *Honey Fitz* cruised alongside, carrying family members and friends, who cheered one or the other of the astonishingly intense racing captains.

On our boat, Ted Kennedy was a virtual Captain Ahab, utterly engrossed in his goal, barking orders in a rudely commanding voice. For me, the orders might as well have been in Swahili. And as Robert's boat began, slowly, to inch ahead of ours, Ted became even more unbearably agitated.

"Set the spinnaker! Set the spinnaker!" he yelled to me furiously at one point.

"The spinnaker?" I repeated phonetically a word I couldn't remember ever having heard before.

"That line, there, for Christ's sake!" Ted Kennedy shouted with impatience, pointing toward the rope that would lift the sail in question from its basket.

"Line?" In Oklahoma, we called a rope a rope.

"Line! Line! That one in the bow. The spinnaker's in the basket!"

I lurched first one way and then another, trying to follow his pointing and his increasingly impatient and unintelligible instructions. His face grew redder and redder. "Can't you see they're getting ahead of us?" he shouted.

As Ted became even more frantic, I wondered seriously whether there was any federal penalty for mutiny on a private sailing vessel. At one point, he yelled toward the *Honey Fitz,* motioning wildly, "Move off! Move off! You're in our wind!"

Our boat did not win the race. Back on shore, over cocktails that evening, I tried to make jokes about the experience, but there had really been nothing very funny about it.

The next day, I sailed as a member of Robert Kennedy's crew in a Hyannis Yacht Club race. Robert's son Joe, and a young friend of Joe's, were also in the crew. Robert proved to be both a daring sailor and a patient captain. On the leg going out, he explained that I would have the job of handling the spinnaker when it was set on the inbound, downwind leg of the race. He showed me how to hold the spinnaker line, once the sail was up, and how to fly the sail like a kite, keeping it full of air.

It seemed odd to me that when every other boat had turned and begun to reach, crosswind, Robert kept going out to sea. He said we'd catch the incoming tide and the wind just right when we headed back toward the bay and the finish line. And his knowledge of the tides and wind, and his skill and daring, paid off. When at last we headed home, running before the wind, we really moved. We set the spinnaker, and this huge, ballooning blue-and-white-striped sail billowed out in front of us. Under Robert's encouragement, I kept the spinnaker full, and we sliced past the other boats, which were still tacking, and won the race with yards and yards of blue water to spare.

His work done, Robert gave the wheel to young Joe, stripped off his shirt and shoes, and jumped off the stern of the boat into the cold bay water, holding onto a trailing rope. He yelled for me to join him, and I was foolish enough to do so.

Clinging to the end of the dragline, Robert and I were pulled headlong through the surging, foamy bay waters behind the boat, which was still under full sail. Then, responding nimbly to a cry from the crew that we were coming into a cluster of jellyfish, Robert moved hand over hand up the rope, against the force of the water, and neatly climbed into the boat with no great trouble. It took me twice as long, and I needed a little help at the last. For several minutes after I had finally reached the security of the deck, I lay there panting, pondering the trials of an underachiever. And I was glad that I had not been born a competitive Kennedy.

Competitive as they were, the Kennedys had an attractive closeness. You can't think about Robert Kennedy without thinking also of the members of his family. They constituted for him an enveloping and almost self-sufficient environment of warmth, loyalty, and enjoyment. Robert Kennedy's brother and sisters appeared to be his best friends, and he theirs. He laughed and teased with them but he trusted them and their judgment, and they were equally and confidently dependent upon him.

When I first knew the Kennedys, Joseph Kennedy was still a central figure in the family, despite the stroke which had silenced him and left him paralyzed. The old man's eyes still saw everything, and he could move his left hand—only a little, but with considerable and varying expressiveness. He could not talk, or get around on his own, and it was difficult to imagine him as the brusque, domineering, aggressive figure described by earlier news reports and biographies. But you could catch some indication of what Joseph Kennedy might have been from the way Robert and Ted treated him. There remained a great deference in their manner toward Joseph Kennedy, and evidence of a touching love. When we were in Hyannis Port, Robert would always slip away from the rest of us just before dinner—and Ted did the same, I understand—to visit his father and carry on a kind of one-sided conversation with him for nearly an hour.

In Hyannis Port, a kind of sibling rivalry existed among the Kennedys concerning which one had invited the most interesting weekend guests. Eunice Shriver generally lost, other family members said, because being seriously involved in the field of mental retardation and related subjects, she was likely to bring with her an entourage of relatively stodgy doctors and psychologists.

LaDonna and I always stayed with Robert and Ethel on these weekends. Their white clapboard house, much like the larger house of his parents next door, was in the center of the "Kennedy compound." At the end of the day, the brothers and sisters and their guests would generally gather at Robert's, or Eunice's, or Ted's, or Jean's, or Pat's for cocktails and fun, and then return to the separate houses for dinner.

On our first trip to Hyannis Port, LaDonna and I met Jacqueline Kennedy at dinner at Robert's house. She had a kind of withdrawn, wistful manner, and she spoke quietly, with a little-girl breathlessness that reminded me of Marilyn Monroe. As soon as I had been introduced to her, she said, "I am so glad to meet you, because you're the man who defeated Bud Wilkinson." Ribbing Robert good-naturedly in the process, Jacqueline and Ethel then told us that they had not shared the obsession of Robert and John with big-time college football, and had kept trying to get both men to see that Wilkinson, whom the president had appointed head of the national physical-fitness program, was a rigid and disloyal conservative. "Ethel and I kept trying to figure out how to get Jack to see this," Jacqueline said. "We even considered writing him an anonymous letter about it, but then Wilkinson finally resigned to run for the Senate, and the problem took care of itself." LaDonna and I found it odd—and sad—that Jacqueline

Kennedy had been unable or unwilling to speak to her husband directly.

I thought Robert Kennedy was a little *too* fond of dogs. I've never been keen on having them in the house. I had a grandfather who was crazy about them—but they were dogs that could hunt. I grew up among people who believed that dogs were supposed to *do* something, and that they were not supposed to live in the same house with humans. In Robert Kennedy's household, there were always at least three dogs underfoot.

The most noticeable of the dogs was Brumus, a black New-foundland almost as big as a Shetland pony. Brumus evidently thought of himself as a small puppy, for he bounded around a living room like one, despite his woolly-mammoth size. He was the scourge of the neighborhood trash cans in McLean, and once he even sidled up and peed on a woman guest's leg at a Kennedy pet show.

One weekend in Hyannis Port, Brumus clambered into the Kennedy family convertible with a bunch of us who were headed to a local horse show, in which assorted Kennedy and Shriver children had been entered. At the show, parents and other human spectators stayed *outside* the fence, but not Brumus.

Brumus apparently preferred the excitement and action in the ring, and he spent most of the time there, to the great annoyance of the somewhat pompous ringmaster. When this official—and some of the horses—could stand the dog no longer, the ringmaster finally undertook to shoo him back outside the fence, using his foot gently to nudge him along. Robert leaped over the fence in an instant and took Brumus by the collar to lead him off, saying in genuine anger, "Don't kick the dog!"

"I didn't kick him," the flustered ringmaster said.

"I saw you, and don't do that again," Robert said icily, white faced.

The rest of us watched, a little embarrassed. And when Robert had led Brumus back to the family group, outside the fence, Jacqueline Kennedy broke the ice by saying, laughingly, "Bobby, there goes the chance any of our children had to win ribbons today!"

The afternoon LaDonna and I sat with Robert and Ethel to hear him read his first major Vietnam speech, Brumus slobbered all over the teacakes.

Art Buchwald once wrote that there was a kind of pecking order for weekend guests at the Kennedy compound in Hyannis Port, with an individual's rank determined by which of the brothers or sisters had invited him. Robert's guests, Art said, ranked highest. They invariably flew back and forth between Washington and Hyannis Port in the Kennedy plane, the *Caroline,* a two-motored prop plane outfitted with a sofa, a work table, and a few individual passenger seats. Buchwald said that guests could get an idea of their rank by seeing whether there was room for them on the *Caroline* for the trip back to Washington at the end of a weekend. If you were Robert's house guest, you always made the *Caroline,* he wrote, but if you were Jean Smith's, say, you couldn't even find out when the plane was scheduled to leave and were reduced to watching carefully for any telltale packing activity in Robert's house.

Robert Kennedy had a genuine and charming rapport with children and young people. He liked to ask them bantering questions. Once, in Tulsa, he and I were on the way to the airport by car when we passed a grade-school playground and all the kids rushed to the fence in an effort to catch a glimpse of him. Robert had the car stopped, and he got out with a bullhorn. "What's the name of this school?" he called out. The kids yelled back their answer. "Do you know who I am?" he asked.

"Yes," they chorused.

"What's my name?"

"Kennedy!" they shouted.

"Do you know who this is with me?" he asked, gesturing toward me.

About half the children yelled "Yes!" and about half yelled "No!"

Robert turned away from the bullhorn and said to me, "I don't see how you ever got elected in Oklahoma."

I remember reading about a similar episode that took place when he was campaigning for president in a town in Indiana, possibly Elkhart. "Are you going to vote for me for president?" Robert called out to a group of grade-school kids.

"Yes!" they yelled back.

"Are you going to get your parents to vote for me?"

"Yes!"

"Have you read my book *To Seek a Newer World?*"

"Yes!"

"You lie in Elkhart, Indiana," he said.

Another time, a very serious young man asked Kennedy, "Do you favor lowering the voting age, and if so, to what level?"

"Yes, I do," Robert answered, "and I think twelve would be about right. After that, I seem to start losing them."

Robert Kennedy understood college students better than did most people at the time of the Youth Revolution of the 1960s. Once, in late 1967, he came to Oklahoma to speak at an Indian youth conference sponsored by an organization LaDonna had founded, Oklahomans for Indian Opportunity; after that, he addressed five thousand wildly enthusiastic University of Oklahoma students in a jam-packed field house. Introduced generously by the university president, George L. Cross, Kennedy alluded in his response to his differences with President Johnson, saying of Cross's introduction, "That's the best thing any president has said about me in a long time."

Kennedy made a brief speech and then opened the huge meeting to questions. One of the first students to get to a microphone asked whether the senator supported automatic draft deferments for college students. Kennedy promptly and firmly stated that he did *not* favor such automatic deferments, particularly so long as some people were unable to attend college because they couldn't afford it. This answer was greeted with general hissing and booing. His answers to other questions invariably brought warm applause and cheers.

"Now let me ask *you* a few questions," Robert Kennedy said at last. "How many of you agree with me about automatic student exemptions from the draft?" Again, there were loud hisses and boos. "How many of you disagree, and think students should automatically be deferred?" Resounding cheers and applause echoed through the barnlike sports arena.

"How many of you want to see a unilateral withdrawal from Vietnam?" A minority.

"How many of you support President Johnson's position on the war—continuing to muddle through?" A slightly larger minority.

"How many of you support my position, calling for a bombing halt and de-escalation?" A somewhat larger group, but still a minority.

"How many of you are for *escalation* of the war?" Very strong applause from at least a plurality, perhaps a majority.

Then, quick as a dart: "How many of you who voted to escalate the war also voted for automatic student deferments?" There was a giant gasp throughout the field house as students realized the inconsistency in their votes, and then an overwhelming tide of applause, partly in approval of his point, partly in admiration for the deft way in which he'd made it.

Afterward, away from the almost hysterical mob of students who had surged around him, seeking to shake hands or just to touch him, I asked Robert whether that was the first time he had used the war and deferment questions, juxtaposed like that, before a student audience. He said that he did it all the time. I also asked him whether the proportions of students voting for the various positions on the Vietnam war were different in Oklahoma from those he had found in other parts of the country. He said they were almost always exactly the same.

Robert Kennedy's antiestablishment pronouncements, his longish hair, and his honest moral fervor made him an authentic hero of young people. But unlike many individuals in the 1960s, he did not romanticize young people as a group. He said that their views on issues, including the Vietnam war, were divided pretty much along the same lines as those of the general population. He was firmly convinced, however, that the minority of students who opposed the war constituted what writer Jack Newfield had called a "prophetic minority," and that they would eventually lead the rest of the country's young people, and help lead the country itself, toward ending America's tragic and immoral Vietnam involvement. And he was right.

Little business was conducted in the Senate on Wednesday, June 5, 1964. Robert F. Kennedy, the junior senator from New York and a Democratic candidate for president, had been shot in Los Angeles, in the early hours of the morning, as he was leaving a celebration of victory in the California Democratic primary. Most Americans were numbed with shock and grief as they watched the television reports of yet another political assassination. LaDonna and I were among them.

But it was not until I went to the Senate chamber on the following day, Thursday, that I finally began fully to realize that Robert Kennedy was really dead. There, I saw that his desk, which was next to mine, had been cleared of all papers; they had been replaced by a small bouquet of flowers. I felt particularly bereft—then, and later at Saint Patrick's, and still later, on the train which brought his body slowly back to Washington—because I mourned as a kind of outsider, not having been among his supporters for the presidential nomination.

"Mr. President," I said, as I rose in the Senate that Thursday, "a small bouquet of pink rosebuds, widow's lace, and fern now rests upon the lonely and vacant desk to my right. It bespeaks the melancholy nature of this day."

There would be no more action pictures of him on television. There would be no more of his sailing at Hyannis Port, or walking along a California beach with his cocker spaniel, Freckles. There would be no more of his coming down to dinner with wet hair after a quick swim. There would be no more of his shy, toothy smile, or quick wit. There would be no more of his righteous outrage, or his passionate "I don't think that's acceptable," or his committed "We can do better."

Except in memory.

7

HHH and
the Politics of Joy

My dad was really surprised, when he first met Vice-President Hubert H. Humphrey, to find that he was not short, dumpy, and pudgy. And during all the time I've known Humphrey, I've been surprised to find how mistaken many people are in the way they perceive him.

For example, far from looking as my father had imagined, Humphrey is slender and trim and rather tall. But this is not the way he is drawn by cartoonists, even now.

Nor is Humphrey the joyful babbler that some comedians still portray him as being.

Hubert Humphrey is, rather, the most important and effective national legislator of this generation. There were flawed years in his career, to be sure—the somewhat humiliating years when he served as vice-president under Lyndon Johnson. But subsequently, unlike many people, he found a chance for renewal, personally and politically. After losing the presidential contest in 1968, Humphrey taught for two years, and then was elected to the U.S. Senate again. There, the old Humphrey blossomed once more—

the Humphrey of the Peace Corps, the war on poverty, the Marshall Plan for the cities.

Hubert Humphrey had come to the Senate in 1948 as something of a pariah. At the 1948 Democratic convention, he had refused to go along with the platform-committee compromise on civil rights, had taken a tough minority plank to the convention floor—and had won. Humphrey had courageously maintained, then, that the Democratic party stood for very little unless it stood for human equality. The majority of the delegates agreed, causing the Southern bloc to walk out. Nevertheless, Harry Truman was re-elected president in 1948. And Hubert Humphrey gained election as a U.S. senator from Minnesota, realizing years of dreams.

Talk about Potomac Fever! No person had ever contracted it more quickly and in more virulent form than did Humphrey. As a young man, he had come to Washington to see his sister, and the effusive letter he wrote at that time to Muriel, later his wife, is almost embarrassing in its statement of his instantly kindled ambition to be elected to Congress.

"Embarrassing" is a word that is easy to use in describing Humphrey—because he and his emotions are all pretty much out in the open. You almost want to look away, sometimes. But "phony" is *not* a word that comes to mind in relation to Humphrey. He is what he is——quick to tears, quick to laughter. When he is sad, he is sadder than anyone else, and when he is joyful, he is happier than the law allows. And mostly, he's joyful.

When Humphrey was a young man, he dropped out of school to help his father in the family drugstore. He stayed home out of loyalty far too long for his own good and his own career. Indeed, this sense of duty to his father almost prevented him from marrying Muriel.

An episode from Humphrey's autobiography, *The Education of a Public Man,* tells a lot about him: When he and Muriel, just married, left for their honeymoon trip, they were accompanied for the first two hundred miles by Humphrey's sister, Frances Howard, because he had agreed to drive her to the place where she could best catch a train back to Washington. One can imagine the newlyweds riding along in the front seat of the borrowed Ford, too embarrassed to say much to each other, with Frances, as bubbly and talkative as Humphrey himself, sitting in the back.

I think of another scene which tells a great deal about Humphrey—this one from the time, following his nomination for vice-president in 1964, when Lyndon Johnson invited him down to the LBJ ranch in Texas. Johnson had Humphrey put on some out-sized cowboy boots, a Western hat, and other Western garb, and get on a horse, in the presence of the national press corps. Johnson himself was not a horseman, no matter what his pose. His personal mount was a specially trained Tennessee walking horse, as easy to ride as a rocking chair. But Johnson had a spirited quarter horse saddled up for Humphrey, whom he knew to be an inexperienced rider, and took a kind of special delight in the resulting discomfiture of his running mate. I can't imagine why Humphrey let the president treat him like that. There's a special poignancy, too, in Humphrey's report in his autobiography about how he reluctantly shot two deer, on that same trip, because Johnson insisted that he do so.

Humphrey came from the tough poverty of South Dakota in the thirties. He knew what it was to see his father powerless, broke, at the mercy of wholesalers and banks and economic conditions generally. If Humphrey had too great a desire to be liked, it must have come from that background.

But many more important traits also came from that background: deep compassion for less fortunate people, a strong conviction that inordinate economic power must be curtailed, an instinctive human warmth and friendliness, a resolution to take pleasure in all of life, including the little things, a steadfast and joyful loyalty to friends, an incurable trust in himself and faith in the improvability of the conditions of life, a Chautauqua speaker's ability to galvanize individuals and whole audiences, a firm belief that determination and hard work always pay off, that virtue *is* its own reward.

Nobody was ever prouder and happier to come to Washington and to the U.S. Senate than was Humphrey. But, as he later told me, he was in for a rude shock. The Senate was at that time a kind of Southern "gentlemen's" club. And there was very little acceptance in it for the man who had caused the Southern walk-out at the Democratic convention.

Humphrey, who wanted more than anything else to be a working, effective senator, a member of the team—who wanted to belong—found himself a rank outsider, an object of ridicule, of ostracism. He told me that on many evenings, during those first months, he actually drove home crying. He said that, one time, as he walked down the center aisle in the Senate chamber and passed the desk of Senate patriarch Richard Russell of Georgia, the most powerful member of that body, he heard Russell say to a nearby colleague, purposely speaking loud enough so that Humphrey would hear, "Why would anyone send a son of a bitch like that to the Senate?"

Perhaps Humphrey tried *too* hard. Perhaps he made too dependent an alliance with Russell's protégé, Lyndon Johnson. But characteristically, he never changed his convictions, and he didn't tailor his advocacy. He did, however, spend a lot of extra time in the senators' private dining room, cultivating Senate leaders. He learned that personal amenities and courtesies were of almost as much consequence as ideology to the Southern senators. He found that socialization—contacts, friendships, helpfulness in little things —was extremely important. And his alliance with Lyndon Johnson provided him with an entree, an opportunity to take advantage of the gift he had for ingratiating himself with others, to employ to good effect his ebullience and his natural desire to be helpful.

Humphrey soon became a leader in the Senate—and when Johnson became president after the assassination of John F. Kennedy, it was natural for him to think of Humphrey as a choice for vice-president.

On the way to the Democratic convention at Atlantic City in 1964, LaDonna and I talked with other Oklahoma delegates about Johnson's possible running mates. The choice had apparently boiled down to two Minnesotans—Hubert Humphrey and Eugene

McCarthy, then Humphrey's colleague in the Senate. LaDonna and I agreed with the other Oklahoma delegates that McCarthy would be preferable. We had long been admirers of Humphrey, though we did not know him personally, but we felt that Senator McCarthy would be a stronger vice-presidential nominee—in the nation as a whole and especially in Oklahoma. He seemed safer, less radical. Ironically, by 1968, just four years later, the roles of Humphrey and McCarthy as representatives of the "safe" and "radical" positions had been reversed.

The first week LaDonna and I were in Washington, Vice-President Humphrey and his wife invited us to dinner at their home, along with three other new senators—Robert Kennedy, Walter Mondale, and Ross Bass of Tennessee—and their wives. On this occasion I saw Humphrey up close, on a really personal basis, for the first time. And it was obvious at once that he was what he appeared to be—open, warm, human—almost too human.

Humphrey is a man of laughter. It is not mean laughter at the expense of others. It is not polite or showy. It is genuine and bubbly—a laughter of enjoyment. We all laughed a lot that first night.

But LaDonna and I didn't arrive at the Humphrey home in a laughing mood. We arrived all out of sorts with each other and fifteen minutes late, having been hopelessly lost two or three times on the way.

Washington is not laid out exclusively as a grid, with the streets all running in one of two directions to form rectangular blocks, like Walters, Oklahoma. Instead, every so often there is a "wagon wheel"—with the hub formed by some such place as Thomas Circle or Dupont Circle, and streets radiating out from it in every direction, like spokes. The layout is confusing for one who grew up in a state where even the rural roads form perfect squares. When my father first came to visit us in Washington, soon after I was elected to the Senate, he could never get his directions straight, and he said one morning at breakfast, "It seems like the sun has come up in a different direction every day I've been here." LaDonna and I knew what he meant.

Muriel Humphrey later told LaDonna and some other women

who were new to the area that the nearest they would come to divorces would be when, driving with their husbands, they got lost in Washington. She said that a map of the city should always be kept in the car, and advised the wives to suggest—as gently as possible, so as not to bruise the man's ego too much—that they stop and ask directions. And we did indeed finally learn to stop and ask.

"Spontaneous." "Fun-loving." Those are two words which apply well to Humphrey. In our early days in Washington, LaDonna became a first-rate tourist guide for Oklahomans who came to visit. We felt especially close to the home-state friends who had worked so hard in my Senate campaign, and we encouraged them to come to Washington, to share a little in our new life in the capital, which they had helped make possible. One time, I organized a charter trip that flew seventy-five of my key people to Washington in a group. LaDonna loved to take visitors through the Capitol. And when Humphrey was in his office there, a ceremonial room just off the Senate floor, he always personally welcomed her and her guests and spent more time with them than he should have.

Frequently, at the end of a work day, Humphrey would invite LaDonna and me to go down with him to his suite in the Executive Office Building, next door to the White House, for a drink and a little conversation. And as likely as not, we would wind up accompanying him during the balance of the evening, wherever he was going. One time, we went with him to meet some Minnesota constituents at the Georgetown Inn, had dinner, and stayed on dancing there until midnight. Humphrey loves to dance; so does LaDonna.

Another time, Humphrey asked us to come along when he dropped by a pre-wedding party for one of his staff members, David Gartner. The affair turned out to be rather formal, and we were seated at the head table and were introduced along with Humphrey as special guests. That night, after most of those attending had left, LaDonna and I and Humphrey, with Gartner and some others, wound up around the piano, joining in familiar old sing-along songs.

Once, LaDonna and I went on an official trip with Humphrey to South Korea, and on the return journey we all stopped over in Alaska for a couple of days, to recover from jet lag and to give the vice-president the opportunity to make a speech in behalf of Senator Ernest Gruening, who was up for re-election. When the political duties were over, we flew to the little town of Seward and settled in at a nearby Air Force recreation camp. There, the next morning, we had wonderful luck at fishing in Resurrection Bay. That night, as we finished eating our catch for dinner and were preparing to head for our separate cabins, Humphrey got word that there was a wonderful old saloon in Seward, with a rinky-tink piano player—and that a few people were dancing there. Humphrey piled us all into our cars, and escorted by the somewhat disconcerted Secret Service men, who had had little time to check out the place, we drove off into the night and descended upon the rustic bar, which, I'm sure, had not seen such activity since the gold rush.

Only four or five people were in the place, including three woman habitues old enough to have been frequenting it since the days of the gold fever. But Humphrey immediately asked one of them to dance, then another, then the third. Word spread through the town that the vice-president of the United States was dancing at the local saloon, and soon the place was packed. Every woman who came in wanted to have a turn dancing with Humphrey, and he did his best to accommodate them all. It was a great night for Humphrey and for the rest of us. And I'm sure that Seward has not been the same since.

"Be of good cheer" is an expression Humphrey uses often. And he means it. His life was tough, when he was growing up. There were disappointments along the way. But "make the best of things" was a creed and a practice that saw him through—just as it did in the case of his recent surgery for cancer of the bladder. He has always been deeply appreciative when good things come his way. He is immensely grateful for friends. And he shows it—as he shows nearly everything else that he feels.

When Humphrey decided to run for president in 1968, after Johnson's withdrawal, his supporters and friends from all around the country put together a mammoth luncheon in his honor at the Sheraton Park Hotel in Washington. I joined with Senator Walter Mondale in chairing the event.

What a crowd! What enthusiasm! Most of those present had been working closely with Humphrey since his earliest days in the Senate, or from the time when he was a founder of Americans for Democratic Action. They had been hoping for perhaps twenty years that he would eventually become president.

And here, at last, he had called them together to announce his candidacy formally! There was a great deal of laughter, some tears, many a standing ovation, and an abundance of wild cheering. It was an exhilarating experience for all those present—and especially for Humphrey.

As usual, he deviated from his prepared text, a carefully worded announcement. (Somebody once called Humphrey a "textual deviate.") In his spontaneous remarks, he referred to a statement originally made by John Adams, and most lately quoted publicly by his fellow Minnesotan Senator Eugene McCarthy, also a candidate for president—something about "the politics of joy."

Well, the phrase stuck. What Humphrey meant—as McCarthy and Adams himself had meant—was that somber as the issues were, citizen participants in democracy could take joy in their efforts.

But it didn't come out that way. Unfairly, Humphrey's reference to "the politics of joy" was said by some to indicate he was totally insensitive to the dying in Vietnam, the rat bites in the slums, the ravages of poverty, and all the other terrible conditions which existed in America and in the world during the awful sixties.

Vietnam. There's no way around it—Hubert Humphrey was badly wrong about Vietnam, as were so many of us. He was right at first, then wrong, and then wrong too long. David Halberstam, author of *The Best and the Brightest,* once asked me in a private conversation whether I felt Humphrey ever really, personally, supported the Johnson war policy. The implication of the question was that Humphrey only did so publicly, in order to stay in Johnson's good graces.

As I told Halberstam, there is absolutely no doubt in my mind that when Humphrey spoke in support of the Johnson war policy, he was saying exactly what he thought. For he said the same things to me privately. And I don't think Humphrey could ever have been a very good liar; he was too transparent. Maybe some critics of the Vietnam war will think the less of him because he supported the war out of conviction, rather than for political reasons; I'm not offering a defense. But I am saying what I think is true: he *did* become convinced that the Johnson war policy was the correct one.

As is now well known, Humphrey originally opposed the war. He wrote a lengthy memorandum, now part of the public record, telling President Johnson why he believed his Vietnam policy was wrong and ought to be changed. That was the real Humphrey, the Humphrey who had stood up for a strong civil-rights plank at the 1948 Democratic convention, the Humphrey with the right moral and human instincts.

But truth to tell, I suppose you could say it was also the real Humphrey who was wounded and hurt when Johnson ostracized him, denying him access to the White House and involvement in high-level decisions, after receiving his Vietnam memorandum. It was the real Humphrey, too, who thereafter went to Vietnam as Johnson's emissary, took at face value the military and other briefings he received there—and came back a convert.

And it was also the real Humphrey, a superb advocate, who began to couch his new support for the Vietnam war—support that was genuine, but perhaps complex and conditional—in fairly simple and colorful public phrases of apparently unconditional approval. It was a bad time for our country and for the Vietnamese. It was a bad time for Humphrey, too.

When Humphrey flew back to Washington from Mexico, following Johnson's announcement of withdrawal from the presidential race, he invited LaDonna and me to come to breakfast with him and Muriel the next morning. On the way there, I warned LaDonna that we should be careful not to encourage him to become a candidate. "Running for president is a very serious business," I said; a person ought to make up his own mind about such a weighty matter. Our job is to help him look at the whole situation as dispassionately as possible and come to the wisest decision. Too, I don't think it's right to advise or encourage him to run if we ourselves are not ready to pledge our full support—and we're not."

The four of us spent a couple of hours, at breakfast and over coffee, looking at his possible campaign for president as carefully as we could. He said that some people, among them George Meany, president of the AFL-CIO, were of the opinion that it was imperative that he announce immediately. Others had warned him that Mayor Richard Daley of Chicago would probably go over to Robert Kennedy unless he announced at once. I told him that in my opinion he had to resist these pressures, that if Daley was going to jump to Kennedy, nothing he did or said could prevent it. I said he ought to ascertain in some detail the kind of support—particularly financial support—he could expect, and that he ought to make an affirmative decision conditional upon receiving concrete, almost contractual, assurances that these obligations would be met. As we left, the promise I made Humphrey was that I would not come to any decision about my own support, as between him and Senator Kennedy, whom he knew to be a very close friend of ours, until he had had plenty of time to decide upon his own course.

LaDonna was crying quietly by the time we got the elevator doors closed. "It just all seemed too cold," she said. "I think he needed more warmth and reinforcement from us."

"But I think we owed him more, out of friendship, than blindly agreeing to his natural inclination to run," I responded.

"I know—and I understand that," LaDonna said. "You're right, I'm sure, but I'm not thinking about the decision or the campaign. I just wish there had been some way we could have let him know how much we like him as a person, and that we're his friends, whatever he decides."

On the spot—that's where LaDonna and I were. Not many Americans have ever had to choose, as we did, between two close personal friends running against each other for nomination as a candidate for president of the United States.

Aided by the advice of our friends and staff in the meeting in my Senate office, we had already pretty much come to the conclusion that if Humphrey decided to run, we would have to support him. But we rocked along for a few days without making any final decision. I did not get to speak to Robert Kennedy, and I had no further conversation with Humphrey, though I knew from what I read in the press and heard from mutual friends that he was moving inexorably toward becoming a candidate.

Then, one day, in the Senate cloakroom, Senator Mondale asked me to join with him as co-chairperson of the Sheraton Park Hotel luncheon at which Humphrey would formally announce. Mondale's invitation sealed my own personal decision.

Fritz Mondale, Robert Kennedy, and I had been seatmates from our very first day in the Senate. I sat in the middle, Kennedy was to my right, and Mondale was to my left. At first, ranking at the very bottom in seniority, we sat in a back row. Subsequently, as we gained seniority, the three of us moved forward as a unit. After Robert Kennedy's death, Senator Mondale and I continued as seatmates.

LaDonna and I and our children and Fritz and Joan and their children were close. We once took a house together for a week at a Delaware beach. We each helped out with meeting and entertaining the constituents of the other. We collaborated on legislation—such as the proposals leading to the creation of a national social-accounting system (Mondale's bill) and of the Kerner Commission (my bill).

Fritz has a well-honed sense of humor, which sometimes has a bite to it. Much of what he says is one-liner, inside stuff, hard to quote, hard to make funny when it is repeated. But sitting between Fritz Mondale and Robert Kennedy in the Senate meant that I joined in a lot of giggling.

One time, at a meeting, LaDonna and I and Joan and Fritz were standing together near the entrance door. Frequently, other entering guests knew me and not Fritz, and I would immediately introduce him, saying, "I want you to know my good friend Senator Walter Mondale of Minnesota." Just as often, a guest knew Fritz and not me, and it would be his turn to say, "I want you to know my good friend Senator Fred Harris of Oklahoma."

Before long, this became a kind of game. When a person knew me and not Fritz, he would say, "That's two points for you"—and vice versa. We were about even on points until Katharine Graham, the publisher of the *Washington Post* and *Newsweek,* came in. LaDonna and I knew her well. "Well, this clinches the title for me," I said to Fritz under my breath.

"Who's that?" he asked. I told him.

Ms. Graham recognized me and extended her hand. "How are you, *Frank?*" she said to me warmly.

"That's *minus* two points," Mondale said.

In accepting Mondale's invitation to join with him in chairing Humphrey's announcement luncheon I had of course made a commitment to support Humphrey. The fact that Mondale had asked me made it easier. And the next step was easier still.

Soon after Humphrey's announcement, Mondale asked me to become national co-chairperson, with him, of the entire Humphrey-for-president campaign. I agreed to do so—and had soon plunged into the job wholeheartedly. LaDonna became just as deeply involved in the campaign, as did our oldest daughter, Kathryn.

But before we took on our formal duties, Mondale and I flew down to Key Largo, Florida, where Humphrey was vacationing, to talk with him in some detail. LaDonna went with me. On the way, Mondale—who had been active in Humphrey campaigns since he was eighteen years old—said that the two of us should obtain a clear understanding with Humphrey about whether we were really to run the campaign or just to serve as figureheads. He said that Humphrey campaigns tended to split up under several leaders.

In our meeting in Key Largo, Humphrey declared that he wanted Mondale and me actually to run things. And we set out to do so. I think, now, it was probably a mistake for Humphrey to choose us to head his campaign, except in name. Both of us, being senators, were burdened with other duties and with obligations to our own constituents. We really didn't have the time necessary to take firm control of the campaign, but we tried.

We divided the campaign-management functions between us. Mine included, among others, administrative oversight of the organization and efforts to secure delegates, and I brought in Robert McCandless, a former Oklahoman and a Washington attorney, brother of Bill McCandless, to head the latter. I told McCandless to read Theodore White's *The Making of the President, 1960,* and to set up a delegate operation similar to the one which had proved so successful for John F. Kennedy. McCandless did so—and well. But the first weekly meeting of the McCandless group was a disaster. McCandless was still trying to learn his job. The whole Humphrey effort had hardly had time to shake down, and we were still having to depend upon many people who had been involved in the Johnson campaign. In that first meeting of the McCandless group, some Johnson operative, reporting on the situation in West Virginia, told us that we should follow through on his earlier promise to deliver $45,000 in cash to a couple of West Virginia politicians, and he added, almost casually, that both of these worthies, now Humphrey supporters, were under indictment by grand juries. Mondale literally exploded, leaping out of his chair, shouting to the Johnson man, "Get out of this room! Out! Out!" Then Mondale turned to McCandless, and almost foaming at the mouth, he said, "I don't *ever* want to hear that kind of talk again." We never did. Some people involved in the Humphrey campaign came to call me and Mondale "the Gold Dust twins" and "the Boy Scouts."

But from the first, there were really two or three separate Humphrey campaigns. There was one run by some of Humphrey's more conservative staff members, such as Bill Connell, and by leftover operatives from the Johnson campaign, such as Richard Maguire (who had also been active in John Kennedy's campaigns). There was another run by old Minnesota friends of Humphrey's, such as Secretary of Agriculture Orville Freeman, trucker Robert Short, and attorney Max Kampelman. And there was the supposedly official campaign which Mondale and I organized and led.

It was a mess. Humphrey struggled forward, making his speeches and appearances, working inhuman hours, and all the time, he was carrying with him the bulky and heavy burden of several duplicative campaign organizations.

Just prior to the 1968 Chicago convention, Mondale, McCandless, and I agreed on a way for making sense out of the campaign organization, or lack of organization. Lawrence O'Brien was brought in as the campaign czar and was given an office in the Executive Office Building, immediately next to Humphrey's own, so that nobody could come between him and the candidate. The change resulted in marked improvement—but we were never able totally to put together the separate campaigns.

I had originally thought that if Humphrey was the nominee, he would probably need to consider someone other than me for his running mate—someone from a populous state, someone from the Kennedy camp, perhaps a Catholic. But as the time of the convention approached, my name figured more and more prominently in speculation about the vice-presidential nomination. There was considerable mention of me in the news magazines *Time* and *Newsweek*. I found this speculation embarrassing, because I was worried that some people might think that my support for Humphrey was connected with my desire to be vice-president.

So, one night at the Pierre Hotel in New York, LaDonna and I sat up late talking about the matter, and concluded that I should remove myself from consideration. Our decision was made in part, too, because we had seen what the office had done to Humphrey, under Johnson. We then called our daughter Kathryn, in Washington, and told her about it. She agreed.

The next day, on the way back to Washington, I thought about how to make my withdrawal believable and final; and I decided that I should endorse another person—Senator Edmund Muskie of Maine.

After leaving our plane, LaDonna and I went directly to Humphrey's office to pose for pictures for a *Look* magazine article. When the photographers had left, Humphrey said to me, "Fred, I have not discussed the vice-presidential nomination with you before, but I want to, now."

I interrupted him. "LaDonna and I decided last night that I should take myself out of the running," I said. I told him that I really meant it, and that I intended to underscore my decision by endorsing another person in an appearance I had scheduled on the ABC "Joey Bishop Show."

Before I could tell him the name of the person I expected to endorse, Humphrey stopped me. "Don't do that, Fred," he said. "I kept you on privately here to tell you that you are one of four people that I'm still seriously considering for the vice-presidential nomination. Don't take yourself out of it. I want to be sure that you understand that I'm making no commitment to you. And I'm not playing any games with you, as Johnson did with me in 1964. I am seriously considering you. Go on out to California for the 'Bishop Show,' and make as good an impression as you can. That will help you, and it will help me. And we'll see what happens."

Our plan had ended almost before it had begun. And, frankly, LaDonna and I found ourselves a good deal more interested, now, in the vice-presidential nomination. I made the appearance on the "Joey Bishop Show"—and received good reviews. Then we went on to the Democratic convention in Chicago, knowing that Humphrey's choices had narrowed down to Governor Richard Hughes of New Jersey, former Peace Corps director Sargent Shriver, Senator Edmund Muskie—and me. There was also some peripheral and less serious consideration of Terry Sanford, a former governor of North Carolina. I got this information not from Humphrey, but from partisans of mine within his staff and from some others among his closest friends and advisers.

And shortly after the convention began, I learned that the list of those being seriously considered by Humphrey for the vice-presidential nomination had been narrowed to two names—mine and Muskie's.

Lawrence O'Brien, in *No Final Victories,* has written that in July, 1968, prior to the Democratic convention in Chicago, he met with Humphrey to discuss Vietnam. "Hubert read me a statement he said he would soon be making public. In it, he favored a bombing halt and a negotiated end to the war. It satisfied me, and I agreed to join his campaign through the Convention." At about the same time, Senator Mondale and I had also listened to and approved the same speech, which Humphrey told us had largely been written by Asian expert Edwin Reischauer.

Just before we left Humphrey's office on that occasion, Senator Mondale asked the vice-president whether he would have to clear the speech with President Johnson. He told us that he would *not* have to clear it, because he would be making this statement as a presidential candidate, not at the incumbent vice-president. He did say that he intended to inform Johnson of the general content of the speech.

Unfortunately, that speech was never given. "About a week later Humphrey visited Johnson at the ranch and on his return, he told me that the President had advised him of a major new development on Vietnam," O'Brien wrote in his book. "Naturally, he said, he should not make any statement until after the President had made his announcement. He added that for security reasons he couldn't reveal the details, but he indicated that the President was about to take a step that would please the anti-war people. That was the last I heard of Humphrey's statement, and his position on Vietnam was to haunt us throughout the Convention and campaign."

I felt I ought to do something. So in a press conference in Puerto Rico, where LaDonna and I had gone to visit Native Americans training for the Peace Corps, I announced my own support for an unconditional bombing halt, de-escalation, and a negotiated settlement of the United States involvement in Vietnam.

My statement made more news around the world and in Paris, the site of Vietnam peace talks, than it did in the United States. It did make news in Oklahoma, however: because of it, I became the only member of the Oklahoma congressional delegation who was publicly opposed to the Johnson policy.

Our ambassador in Paris, the venerable diplomat Averell Harriman, later sent encouraging word to me through Bill Moyers, a former Johnson aide, to the effect that my statement was on the right track and that I should persist in my position in order to help move the Johnson administration in the right direction.

But in the Humphrey campaign itself there had been no public effort, by the time of the Chicago convention, to differentiate between the vice-president's views on Vietnam and the Johnson war policy. "I believed . . . that to be elected Humphrey had to disassociate himself from Johnson's Vietnam policy," O'Brien states in his book. "Harris and Mondale agreed, but we were by no means a majority in the Humphrey circle of advisers." That was true.

A part of my job at the convention—since Larry O'Brien had taken over direction of the Humphrey campaign itself—was to work with Washington attorney David Ginsberg on the platform. A peace plank was drafted, using almost the exact words that Senator Edward Kennedy had employed in a speech at Worcester, Massachusetts, just prior to the convention, calling for an unconditional bombing halt, de-escalation, and a negotiated settlement. Humphrey approved the plank, and O'Brien and Ginsberg and I began the task of selling it to key Democratic leaders. Then, some of President Johnson's people blew up our coalition in the platform committee and among delegates generally by deciding to oppose the Humphrey peace plank openly.

When that happened, late one night, David Ginsberg and Humphrey staffer William Welch came and asked my advice. "It's time for some moxie," I told them firmly, using the word I had learned from Robert Kennedy. I told them that Humphrey should stand firm for the peace plank. "If Johnson opposes it, that's his business," I said. "I believe Johnson will back down, but even if he doesn't, Humphrey will have done the right thing, and he will have made his break with Johnson."

There was a rather long silence. David Ginsberg and Bill Welch sat there awhile, and then they asked me what my fallback advice was. I said I didn't have any. They left to discuss the situation with Humphrey.

Unfortunately, the Humphrey group decided upon a "compromise" peace plank, watering down the language which had previously been agreed upon. Bill Welch asked me to lead the effort for adoption of the compromise plank, but I refused, and Senator Muskie and Representative James O'Hara of Michigan took on the responsibility for pushing it through. It was adopted by the convention, but at great cost, with the divisions within the party widened, and the day delayed when Humphrey would have to break openly with the Johnson war policy.

I do believe that prior to the convention, Humphrey had begun to change his mind about the Vietnam war, and was moving back toward something near his original position. And I do not believe he delayed saying so publicly out of any fear of Johnson's wrath, or because of political considerations. My judgment is that Humphrey was told by senior administration officials, probably including the president himself, that peace in Vietnam was nearly at hand and that any statement by him criticizing existing United States policy would weaken and perhaps ruin the chances for the negotiations to succeed.

On the night Humphrey received the Democratic nomination, he began more open and serious conversations with advisers and supporters about the choice of a running mate. Outside, there were demonstrations and violence in the streets and terrible misuse of force by the Chicago police. LaDonna had been invited to watch the balloting for the presidential nomination with Humphrey and some of his closest staff people in the Humphrey hotel suite upstairs. Our daughter Kathryn, our son, Byron, and I had intended to watch it on television from my office at the convention center. Instead, we spent most of the evening looking at television reports of what was happening in the streets—and crying, all three of us.

Back at the hotel, much later, when the streets were quiet and our children had gone to bed, LaDonna and I received periodic reports from friends in the Humphrey suite about how the selection of a vice-presidential nominee was going. We heard that Humphrey had called in the mayor of Pittsburgh and the mayor of Philadelphia. One had voiced support for Muskie, the other for me. We were informed that labor leaders he had consulted had also been equally split in their recommendations. Finally, a friend came to tell us that Humphrey had gone to bed at about four o'clock in the morning with the decision still not made.

Dead tired, LaDonna and I didn't awaken the next morning until half past ten. Since I knew Humphrey had previously scheduled a press conference for ten o'clock to announce his choice of a running mate, I assumed he had selected Muskie. I must say that I felt some relief at this point. I was heartsick about the insensitivity shown toward the demonstrators by the Daley police and by too many of the Johnson people, who were in rigid control of the convention. I was disappointed that Humphrey had not stuck with the original peace plank.

But I had not lost interest in the vice-presidential nomination. The interest was still there, and it was rekindled when, in a little while, a report came from the Humphrey suite that no decision had yet been made and that the scheduled press conference had been postponed.

Close friends began to gather in our hotel room, to wait with us. Hour by hour, the discussion continued upstairs, and hour by hour, the press conference at which Humphrey was to announce his running mate was delayed.

At one point, a young aide assigned to me came bursting into the room to announce, "It must be you! The Secret Service are here on this floor!" I sent someone to check out his report and found that he had mistaken a couple of hotel security people for Secret Service agents.

We resumed our vigil, amidst a lot of laughter among all of us in the room, which eased the tension. Suddenly the same young aide returned to say, "This time, I know the Secret Service people are on this floor! I asked one to show me his identification." Again I sent someone to check out the report, and again the optimism in the room faded, when the scout returned to say that the Secret Service people were there only because Muriel Humphrey was preparing to attend a meeting on our floor.

At last, the phone rang. It was Humphrey, asking me to come up to his suite. I left the hushed group of well-wishers and speeded up the stairs.

Humphrey greeted me at the door and took me through an anteroom, where a number of his staff people were waiting, and into a bedroom. Our conversation was very brief. He told me that he'd narrowed the choice down to me and Muskie. We discussed the vice-presidential nomination, the office of vice-president, and the qualities and qualifications I might bring to the campaign and to the office itself. I frankly don't remember very much of this conversation.

Humphrey then asked me to wait while he went into another

room. Soon he came back and talked to me some more. Then he left again to go into the other room. When next he returned, he put his hand on my shoulder and with tears welling up in his eyes, he said, "Fred, I'm going to have to choose the older man."

I said, "If that's your decision, I'll be glad to nominate Ed Muskie."

"Would you really?" he asked. I said that I certainly would. He then asked me to accompany him into the other room to notify Senator Muskie of his decision. I realized then that we had been in adjoining bedrooms and Humphrey had been shuttling back and forth between us.

Humphrey and I walked into the other bedroom. There stood a somewhat nervous Senator Muskie, leaning on a bureau. In what was probably one of the longest sentences the tall Maine senator had ever heard, Humphrey said, "Ed, shake hands with the man who is going to nominate you."

I congratulated Ed, and he and I left immediately. He had to get ready for the press conference. I had to notify my friends and start working on my nominating speech. Ironically, a few minutes after I returned to my hotel room, a representative of the Secret Service appeared breathlessly to ask whether I knew Senator Muskie's room number.

That night I stood before the convention and nominated Ed Muskie. I was proud to do so. He is a good, solid man, and he was an asset to the ticket. I'm also proud that I took the occasion of that nominating speech to express my disapproval of the conduct of the Chicago police.

LaDonna and I returned to Oklahoma. For several weeks after the convention, our participation in the campaign was slight. As a matter of fact, our hearts hadn't been in it much since the assassination of Robert Kennedy. Robert McCandless arranged for me to have a desk and secretary at the offices of the Democratic National Committee; technically, Senator Mondale and I were still the national co-chairpersons of the Humphrey-Muskie campaign, although we had not had day-to-day administrative responsibility for it since Larry O'Brien had been brought in, prior to the convention. Following Humphrey's nomination, O'Brien became head of the Democratic National Committee, and he continued to direct the campaign.

I made speeches and other appearances when asked, and I took part in the policy meetings. It was obvious that the campaign was in deep trouble. For one thing, the administration of its several facets was still fragmented, despite O'Brien's over-all responsibility. One group, under Secretary of Agriculture Orville Freeman was responsible for scheduling and publicizing campaign events, while another group, under Robert McCandless, who reported directly to O'Brien, was responsible for the organization of support at various levels and for getting out the vote. Frequently, the local operatives of these two units did not communicate with each other. Fund raising was going very poorly. And there was general despair, a feeling that the campaign was hopeless.

One of the few who did not think it was hopeless was Humphrey himself. His courage was heroic, and his efforts were Herculean. He kept going doggedly on, against all the odds. And he almost pulled it out.

A turning point in the campaign was his nationally televised speech on Vietnam. As soon as Humphrey had agreed to make this major policy address, Larry O'Brien asked me to join the staff in the campaign airplane, so that I could help Humphrey write the speech and could use my influence to get him to embody in it a clear differentiation between his own Vietnam policy and Johnson's. This was to be his last chance to do so.

LaDonna and I flew to Los Angeles, met with Humphrey, and then went on with him and the traveling entourage of campaign-staff and press people to Sacramento, San Francisco, Portland, Seattle, and finally, Salt Lake City.

All along this route, the inner-circle debate between the supporters of the Vietnam war and those who opposed it grew hotter and hotter. At each stop, suggested drafts and redrafts of the Vietnam speech were teletyped back and forth between the Humphrey entourage and the campaign headquarters in Washington. Before long, each side in the debate brought up reinforcements. On the peace side, Larry O'Brien himself joined the group in the plane, as did Bill Welch and former State Department official George Ball.

Incredibly, the debate was still going on and still unresolved when a late-night meeting broke up in Salt Lake City on the very evening before the speech was scheduled to be taped. And it was still going on the next morning, up until thirty minutes before the speech had to be typed for the TelePrompTer.

I was frankly disappointed in the final version which Humphrey decided upon. It didn't go far enough to suit me. Also, the three most important paragraphs were mutually inconsistent. The first of these seemed to call for a bombing halt without preconditions. But the next paragraph stated that the "other side" ought to be willing to take certain steps *first*. And the third paragraph declared that if we stopped the bombing and the other side didn't respond, the force we would then use would be greater than ever.

LaDonna and I sat in the studio as Humphrey taped the speech. Soon after the taping was finished, the Salt Lake City station began to feed it to the network for immediate broadcasting. At this point, Humphrey left the viewing room to make a telephone call. It's my impression that the call was to President Johnson. When Humphrey came back, his face was ashen. I imagine that the call had not been a very easy one to make, and my guess is that Johnson did not take very kindly to receiving Humphrey's report on the content of the speech after it was already being broadcast throughout the nation.

LaDonna and I rode back from the television studio to the hotel in the press bus, so that we could get the reactions of the reporters. We found that there was considerable disagreement among them. Some said the speech was a mere rehash of previous Humphrey statements. Some said it was a reiteration of the Johnson line. Some thought it represented an unmistakable break with Johnson's war policy.

But by the time we got back to the hotel, we already had the news that Senator Edward Kennedy had hailed the speech as a very good one, and had said he was now willing to pledge his full-fledged support of the Humphrey candidacy. That action started the flood of endorsements from political figures who up until that time had been hanging back.

It was soon clear that the Humphrey speech came across to the television audience as a call for a change in the Vietnam war policy; viewers understood it to be a "peace" speech—and to a great extent it was. In any event, the campaign began to catch fire from that moment—and the televised speech itself brought in twice as much money in contributions as it had cost to broadcast.

Soon, Humphrey was no longer campaigning alone. More and more politicians were willing to be seen with him. Experienced observers began to feel that the campaign might just possibly be successful. President Johnson and Governor John Connally of Texas put on a huge rally for Humphrey in Texas, bringing together all elements of the Texas Democratic party.

On the night before the election, LaDonna and I flew out to Los Angeles to take part in a nationally televised telethon. A downtown parade in Los Angeles brought out one of the largest crowds ever seen for a candidate there. Thousands thronged the streets to cheer as Humphrey's caravan passed by. And a respected California poll, the Field poll, that day indicated that Humphrey had pulled even with Nixon in California.

Our campaign telethon could not have gone over better. Spirits were high. After the telethon, we went to a party at the Beverly Hills home of Lloyd and Ann Hand, who had erected a giant tent in their backyard. A wonderful crowd of friends and supporters, movie stars and political figures, attended. There was excellent food and music, and the dancing continued until the early hours of the morning.

Finally, we went in a caravan to the airport and boarded the campaign plane for Minnesota. Immediately upon landing, Humphrey and Muriel went to vote. The rest of us checked in at the Leamington Hotel for a few hours of sleep.

On election night, as the returns began to come in, it was soon clear that the best Humphrey could expect was a no-majority deadlock in the Electoral College, which would leave the decision up to the U.S. House of Representatives. That prospect seemed no better to me than defeat.

But defeat there was. And Humphrey's defeat was awfully sad for all of us who had been involved in the campaign, especially because we admired the way he had worked his heart out—never giving up during the days of abuse by peace demonstrators, of despair about the public-opinion polls, of humiliation when various public officials had declined to be seen with him.

"We were with him at the first and we ought to go down and stand with him at the last," I told a tearful LaDonna. She fixed her face, we joined Humphrey and Muriel, and together with Senator Mondale and other close friends and family members, we walked into the Leamington ballroom. It was tough for all of us to keep the tears out of our eyes. Humphrey made a good concession statement, and it was all over.

Except for the plane ride back to Washington, which was much like an Irish wake. Humphrey stayed on in Minnesota. The rest of us flew back together, and almost everyone on board alternated between singing, and laughing, and crying. At the airport, we shook hands and embraced, some of us never to see each other again, and most of us never again to be as close.

Humphrey was not the best *possible* candidate for president, but perfect candidates don't exist, or if they do, they don't run. I was proud to be associated with him. I could never understand the attitude of some liberals, during that campaign, who said that it would really make no difference whether Humphrey or Richard Nixon was elected. I used to tell them that there would be at least one important difference—in the kind of Supreme Court members that would be appointed during the next four years.

I was glad that I didn't have to have Richard Nixon's election on my conscience.

After Humphrey's defeat by Nixon in 1968, Lawrence O'Brien stepped down as head of the Democratic party. I wanted to heal the terrible divisions in the party, so, with Humphrey's blessing, I talked with every single member of the Democratic National Committee, some of them a number of times, telling them of my plans for the party and soliciting their support. I was chosen to succeed O'Brien by unanimous vote.

One reporter likened my wanting to chair the Democratic party to parachuting onto the *Titanic*. But I had been deeply troubled about not having done more, earlier, to help end the war in Vietnam. I had also felt awfully uncomfortable before the 1968 election about finding myself joined, in support of the same candidate, with opponents of what I believed was needed party reform. I wanted to have a chance to make amends and to help put the party back together again as a vehicle for helping put the country back together again.

So, I sought the job—and got it. I appointed the Democratic Policy Council, which took a strong stand against the war and placed the party squarely on the human side of social, economic, and civil-rights issues. I appointed the McGovern Commission, which reformed the undemocratic delegate-selection process, and the O'Hara Commission, which reformed the archaic party rules.

It was no walkover, as they say. The job was a kind of balancing act. And I came to believe that there was some immutable natural law which required every committee to have at least twenty-one members. Each time I set up a committee, I would try to hold down the number of members—but I couldn't do it. Reformers had to be balanced with establishment Democrats in such a delicate manner as to insure a reform result, but one which could both merit and win the eventual approval of the establishment-oriented Democratic National Committee. And, too, male members of such committees had to be balanced with females, young members with older members, white and Anglo members with minority members, national officials with state and local officials, Northerners with Southerners and Easterners with Westerners. Inexorably, during the appointing process, the number of committee members would begin to creep upward, toward the immutable twenty-one. And invariably, shame to tell, someone would say something like, "We're still short on blacks, young people, women, and mayors; does anybody know someone who fits all four categories—or even three?"

The worst part of my job as head of the Democratic party was trying to raise money. I could make no progress toward reducing the debt, but in those virulently divisive times it was no little accomplishment, I thought, just to keep the party on its feet—to pay the rent, salaries, and phone bills—while we rehabilitated it, and I did bring in a full-time expert who started the party on the small-givers program which ultimately became its main financial base.

Being head of the Democratic party hurt me badly in Oklahoma. Too many people resented my taking on a job other than the one to which they had elected me. And my new, more partisan image was a hindrance to me, both at home and in the Senate.

So, when I could—when I was sure the party was locked into its new directions—I stepped out of the job, and the once and future chairman, Lawrence O'Brien, stepped back into it again.

While the party was achieving renewal, so was Humphrey, and he gained re-election to the Senate from Minnesota two years after having been defeated in the 1968 presidential election. In many ways, he began to seem to be the old Humphrey of Senate days again. Then, someone talked him into seeking the nomination for president in 1972. Perhaps no talking was necessary; it's hard to get rid of the presidential urge. I know.

Political careers are very dependent upon the vagaries of fate. And in Humphrey's case, fate always seemed to dictate bad timing. He should not have run in 1972. He should have helped McGovern, as I did after I was out as a candidate that year. Instead, he not only ran but let himself get talked into a bitter, last-ditch, stop-McGovern effort at the Democratic convention in Miami Beach, an effort which hindered the healing of Democratic lesions and helped to seal the doom of the McGovern campaign from the first.

Some said Humphrey *should* have run in 1976. I don't know about that. One reason he enjoyed such popularity and was the object of so much laudatory comment in the press during the 1976 Democratic presidential primaries was precisely that he was *not* a candidate. Had he become a candidate, many of the old critics would probably have begun to work on him again.

In any event, it was a sad occasion when Humphrey finally announced that he would not be a presidential candidate in 1976.

The statement amounted to an end, at last and forever, of his presidential ambitions.

Despite the poignancy of the announcement, however, it seemed to me that Humphrey was taking the wise and correct course. As I listened, I thought about the five outstanding senators —Daniel Webster, Henry Clay, John C. Calhoun, Robert La Follette, and Robert Taft—and how the careers of most of them were somewhat burdened by an ambition to be president. I was convinced that Humphrey's career would now take on added luster.

For there is a kind of freshness and youthful innovativeness about Humphrey: he has an idea a minute, some have said, and most of the ideas are good ones. The Humphrey-Hawkins bill, for example, requiring government action to bring about full employment, became the most popular proposal in the 1976 presidential campaign, among Democrats at least, and gained the unanimous endorsement of all the major Democratic leaders in the country.

Of course, I never knew Al Smith, whom Franklin Roosevelt called the "happy warrior." But I have always felt that this appellation also suits Humphrey exactly. Humphrey has never failed to move me, in any speech I have heard him make. And he has never failed to make me laugh, if he wanted to, during a speech or in a personal conversation. He is always undaunted and cheerful in the face of adversity, continuing to do the "Lord's work," as he puts it, eyes twinkling.

Humphrey will win you over, and he'll keep trying until he does. Once I had the job of holding a huge, restless crowd in Detroit, when he was an hour late. Humphrey likes people so much that he always finds it hard to tear himself away from the ones he's with. In a long day of scheduled events, the continued delays pile up.

It was hot, that day in Detroit. The room was overcrowded. The microphone was not working properly. But every person present was a Humphrey partisan. They all cheered whenever I mentioned his name. At last—at long last—he finally arrived.

While the crowd's extended applause and cheering roared

around him, I said to him, "They've been waiting about an hour. It's too hot in here and too crowded. The microphone is really bad, and so are the acoustics. Since everyone here's already for you, I think you ought to give them about five minutes only, and wrap it up." He gave me a kind of irritated look, and then went back to smiling and waving to the crowd.

When the cheering had died down, Humphrey began to speak. Shouting to be heard, he began to grow hoarse before he was more than three or four minutes into his remarks. But the crowd listened with great attentiveness. And then Humphrey delivered an applause line, and the applause came in a great and sustained burst. Well, there was no way to cut him short after that! He gave *two* of the best speeches I had ever heard, and the crowd loved every minute of it. Afterward, the first person to get to him from a crushing mass of wildly enthusiatic supporters was a woman who said, "That was the greatest speech I've ever heard!" Humphrey thanked her, and before turning back to the next well-wisher, he raised his eyebrows at me as if to say, "And you, you son of a bitch, you wanted to cut me to five minutes!"

I'm glad that Humphrey is still on the political scene, and that he hasn't been cut short.

8

This, at Least, Was Good

I did not seek re-election to the Senate in 1972. Instead, I ran for president—or, a little more accurately, I took a quick jog. I was a very earnest candidate until I went broke, but that took a surprisingly short time.

Some said I ran for president in 1972 because I knew Oklahomans would not vote me into the Senate again. That is not true. I believed I could be re-elected. My principal Democratic opponent would have been Congressman Ed Edmondson, brother of Howard Edmondson, whom I had defeated in the primaries in my first Senate race. With me out, Ed Edmondson gained the Democratic nomination without opposition, but he then contrived to lose in the general election to a former Republican governor of Oklahoma, Dewey Bartlett, easily the dullest campaigner in the history of the state. Two years later, Edmondson managed to lose narrowly again, this time to the Republican incumbent, Senator Henry Bellmon, recognized as Oklahoma's second dullest campaigner of all time. In both races, Edmondson undertook to out-conservative his opponents. This approach never works, because the voters usually prefer the more genuine article.

I thought I would have won, but it is certainly true that I was a highly controversial figure after eight years in Washington. I had become an outspoken critic of the oil monopolies and their unfair tax privileges. As head of the Democratic party, I had helped push through the reforms which, among other things, stopped the practice by which the Oklahoma party hierarchy *appointed* one-half of Oklahoma's delegates to the national convention. Alone among the members of the Oklahoma congressional delegation, I had broken with President Johnson and President Nixon on the Vietnam war. I had been the most ardent advocate of the measures for combating racism recommended in the Kerner Commission report.

My senatorial interests and activities had grown to include a wide span of concerns—from broadening East–West trade to prohibiting the killing of ocean mammals. Comparing Senator Bellmon and me, one editor of a conservative Oklahoma weekly newspaper had written, "Oklahoma has two United States Senators; one doesn't do anything, and the other does too damn much."

But I decided against running again for the Senate because LaDonna and I would have had to spend a whole year of our lives doing nothing but campaigning, and I did not think it was worth it. I had already been in the Senate for eight years, and—in truth—I did not think the country had been changed for the better very much, if at all, during that period. I mean no disrespect to that great body when I say that people who have never served in the Senate tend to overrate its power. My first years in the Senate were growing, stretching, exhilarating years. But as I became increasingly frustrated, I began to feel that it was time to get out of the way and let someone else try for a while. And I thought that even a *campaign* for president could help move the country in the right direction.

But I had grossly underestimated the difficulty of raising money to finance a campaign focused on the goal of fairly distributing wealth, income, and power. Too, I had waited far too long to announce; Senator George McGovern and others, I found, had long since secured for themselves much of the backing and support I had hoped to count on.

So I went broke rather quickly in the campaign for the 1972 Democratic nomination for president—and pulled out even before the first primaries. David Broder, of the *Washington Post,* wrote that it was a great shame that the only reason Senator Henry Jackson could continue as a candidate, and I could not, was money. Ironically, my withdrawal announcement that year probably received more press attention than did my active campaign. I guess if I could have kept on withdrawing about once a week, I might eventually have caught on.

But the fact was that I did not catch on. So, I finished my Senate term, working for land reform and tax reform and against monopolies and strip mining.

And then I was out. Well, not entirely. Still subject to the basic symptom of Potomac Fever, LaDonna and I lingered on near the shores of that great river. I formed a group called New Populist Action to fight for tax reform, and I became active as a private citizen in a number of other public-interest groups and causes. I began teaching a course of my own devising, "New Populist Studies," at Washington's American University. La-Donna continued as president of Americans for Indian Opportunity, an Indian advocacy organization with headquarters in the nation's capital.

What was it like, being out of the Senate? Our reactions were mixed. We no longer received the most prestigious invitations. To amount to anything in the highest social circles in Washington, one needs a power base; and, too, in my last years in the Senate, I had offended many establishment interests. But LaDonna and I felt almost no sense of loss at the change in our social standing. It had been some years, anyway, since we had been caught up in Washington's social world.

There was, of course, a period of adjustment. I missed having a staff, particularly researchers and stenographers. But once I got back into the habit of doing my own research, I began to take joy in it, as I had not done since I was a student law-review editor.

I had to relearn how to do the most everyday tasks. A wonderfully loyal and mothering private secretary and a number of obsequious and ubiquitous public officials had handled such matters for me for so long that my ability to do them for myself had almost atrophied. How did one go about having a driver's license renewed or securing an automobile-inspection sticker? I had not the slightest idea. It was like getting out of law school and not knowing where the courthouse was. And finding out in each case gave the same sense of accomplishment. I began to make my own lecture bookings and my own arrangements with respect to writing and teaching. I began to carry my own bags, open my own doors, and take care of my own travel schedules and provisions for lodging. Former Supreme Court Justice William O. Douglas was, he wrote, immensely proud of his ability to survive unaided, if need be, in a trackless wilderness. I began to feel something akin to that pride in my revived *everyday* skills.

Moving around without an entourage, more relaxed and in touch with people and the world, less harried and driven, I began to notice that images and sounds and smells and personalities were becoming for me more distinct, less glazed and muffled, less subdued and blurred. The truth really was that I enjoyed being out of the Senate, just as I had for so long enjoyed being in it.

In the spring of 1974, however, I began to think seriously about running for president again. LaDonna urged it. So did two of my best and most trusted friends, Jim Hightower, director of the Agribusiness Accountability Project, and Peter Barnes, West Coast editor of the *New Republic*.

At first, I could not see how it could be done successfully. Instead, I decided to write a long letter to my friend Senator Walter Mondale of Minnesota, then an announced candidate, giving him my soundest advice about what kind of campaign he should run; I expected probably to wind up supporting him as the best person in the race.

A campaign for president is, as we might say down home, like the Fort Worth Fat Stock Show; you have to see one for yourself to know what it is really like. I had done that, and afterward, I

had had time to reflect about it. So, for nearly a month, in between other tasks and while flying back and forth across the
country for meetings and lectures, I worked on the memorandum
to Mondale. At last, I read it aloud one morning to LaDonna
and our daughter Kathryn, who happened to be home from
school. I was stunned when they both said they found it offensive
—not because of the contents, with which they agreed, but because they felt the very idea of such a memorandum was pre-
sumptuous. One must assume, they pointed out, that a person
who has announced for president already possesses some fairly
strong notions about how and why to go about it.

I had to admit that they were right. Yet, I felt that *someone*
had to run for president for the reasons and in the manner I had
outlined. So, with the help of LaDonna and others, I redrafted
the memorandum, no longer addressing it to Mondale, as "A
Model 1976 Presidential Campaign," and had copies printed in
quantity, in June, 1974. Without finally committing *myself* to run,
and not knowing whether the response would be warmly encouraging or raucously mocking, I mailed the memorandum to
several hundred friends and other potential supporters throughout the country, asking for their comments. The responses were
overwhelmingly enthusiastic. Just when I thought I was through
with campaigning at last, I became a candidate once more.

But this campaign was to be different. The issues were crisply
refined from the first. So were the underlying assumptions of the
campaign, the strategy, and the style. All these were stated plainly
in the 1974 memorandum. As the campaign unfolded, we followed that memorandum almost to the letter. And we nearly
made it work.

I had learned, as I said in the memorandum, that "in the
American tradition, the most effective way to raise issues is
through elective politics, and a Democratic presidential campaign
is the best vehicle." Emphasis on this point was particularly necessary, I felt, if I was to have any chance of involving public-
interest activists around the country who had come to feel, with
good reason, that fighting utility companies at the local level—

for example—was a more effective way of using their time and energies than participation in a national campaign. Most of them had seen too many months and too many minds used up in campaigns which went nowhere and left no lasting trace. I hoped this one would be different, and said so.

In August and September, 1974, I held a series of private-home coffees in California and in New Hampshire, asking people to sign written support cards. A majority of those at each coffee did sign them.

Then, and throughout the campaign, the toughest problem was that too many people really did not believe that democracy could be made to work. "You should win, and I hope you do," they would say, "but can you? Will they let you—the party powers and the wealthy and corporate interests?"

I explained how party reforms launched when I was Democratic chairperson had given ordinary people a fighting chance. "If we want to be, you and I *are* the Democratic party," I said, and I reminded them of how McGovern's untrained but committed volunteers had handily beaten the party powers in 1972.

Frequently, that argument settled one point only to raise another. "But look what happened to him," they would say.

I pointed out that the new campaign-financing law—limiting contributions to $1,000 and providing for federal matching funds in the primaries and full federal financing in the general election —had cut down to size the rich and the friends of the rich, and had made it possible for us to put into practice the principle of "one person, one vote." "In the past," I said, "some people had more than one vote, because they had the money."

"A lot of big shots are waiting to see which way the wind is going to blow," I would say toward the end of each gathering, just before asking people to sign support cards. "I'm asking you to *decide* which way the wind will blow. If you say 'I know Fred Harris, he's the best person in this race, I'm for him, and he's going to win'—and you have to say 'He's going to win'—if you say that often enough and strongly enough, you yourself, will make it come to pass." Invariably, at least half of those who heard the message signed up. A gifted staff member, Frank Greer, produced a sound and slide show of the whole presentation by me and LaDonna, and committed supporters throughout the country began, with copies of it, to show the slides and conduct their own coffees, signing up new supporters themselves.

Campaigns consist of two main processes: identifying supporters, and reinforcing their commitment. The support cards, called "green cards" because that was the color of the original batch, were the lifeblood of our campaign. Whipping out a green card and signing up a person who expressed support became second nature for all those in our organization. Staff members and supporters always carried a supply of cards, and everyone in the campaign came to anticipate almost instinctively the exact moment at the end of a coffee when I would say, "Some of my friends will pass out some cards among you."

During the campaign, our older daughter, Kathryn, married Manuel Tijerina. Our other daughter, Laura, now fifteen, was the bridesmaid. As the three of us waited nervously for our time to enter and walk down the aisle of the little Deyo Mission Indian church near our old home town of Lawton, Oklahoma, Laura playfully peeped into the packed sanctuary and then turned back to me and said, "It's a good crowd, Daddy; do you want me to pass out green cards at the end of the ceremony?"

There were two basic assumptions underlying the campaign. As stated in the 1974 memorandum, the first was that "the fundamental ideal of the American experiment is the widespread diffusion of economic and political power"; the other was that "people are smart enough to govern themselves." These fundamental assumptions were stated over and over—in campaign literature and by me at coffees—until everyone could repeat them by rote. This always happens with the words and phrases much employed in a particular campaign, and may cause, among insiders, a kind of giddy and joking use of them, after a while. One night in California, we were rushing between two coffees, following three local supporters in a lead car. After we had backtracked for the third time, they finally stopped under a street light and got out to study a city map. We pulled up beside them, and I called, "Are we lost?"

"No," one answered without looking up, "we're just having a little debate about whether people really are smart enough to govern themselves."

The campaign memorandum said, "People can be expected to do the right thing, to act in their own best interests—if they have the facts and are given real choices." I still think that is true. We proved it over and over by the way people of diverse groups understood and responded to my message. The trouble was, as it turned out, that for various reasons, neither I nor what I had to say was ever heard by enough people.

Mine was an issues campaign from the first. I did not see the presidency as some kind of Man of the Year award. I had already received all the awards a person ought to have. I was interested in being president because I felt deeply about the issues. As I stated in the original memorandum, "Too few people have all the money and power; most people have little or none.

"The campaign must address the real, day-to-day problems of people—heavy and unfair taxes, bad or non-existent housing, inadequate and costly medical care, inflated food, utility and other prices, high interest rates, exhorbitant military expenditures and waste, cynical and interventionist foreign policy, low wages and unemployment—in terms of how economic and political privilege thwarts the will of the people." That is how the memorandum put it.

A deep-seated concern with issues was the reason for the campaign and the basis of our ability to enlist such fervently dedicated supporters. But I found to my surprise that some people who thought of themselves as "issue-oriented" liberals professed more interest in issues at first than they demonstrated later on. In the beginning, some of these were quoted to the effect that they liked what I said, and they agreed that I could stir a crowd, but they wondered about my "depth" on the issues. In due time, forums were set up all around the country, at which the candidates spoke and answered questions on the issues, and when it became apparent that I invariably came off best at these forums, and obtained the most enthusiastic response, some of the same liberals began to say I was *too* good on the issues. "Of course, you're the best on the issues," one sponsor of the issues forums told me when they were over, "but you just can't get elected talking like that, and I'm tired of getting beat."

One wealthy liberal whose principal interest was in breaking up the oil companies, a key part of my own program, expressed the same practical concerns; he would not make a commitment to me because he was afraid I could not win. Later, he endorsed former Governor Jimmy Carter of Georgia, at a time when Carter was the only moderate-to-liberal candidate who had *not* taken a strong stand on curbing oil-company power.

Once, I asked former Senator Eugene McCarthy how he explained the fact that some of those who had been among his most dedicated and reform-minded supporters in 1968 were among Senator George McGovern's most Machiavellian manipulators of credentials and platform issues at the Democratic convention in 1972. "Idealists should be limited by law to involvement in one campaign only," he replied. "After that, they tend to get too interested in power." There is some truth in what he said.

An early problem in my campaign was that I found myself tagged a "radical" by *Time* magazine, Walter Cronkite, and others. They were not being malicious; it's just that they were seeking a label and I am hard to categorize. I am not exactly a traditional liberal. I believe, as Thomas Jefferson did, in the widespread diffusion of economic and political power—it is in these terms that I define New Populism. Such diffusion would require no change in the Constitution or in our basic principles and very little change in our laws. Basically, it would mean putting into practice what we say we believe. So, as I said to every crowd and gathering during the campaign, we ought to have a graduated income tax, rather than graduated loopholes, we ought to break up the monopolies that overcharge us, and we ought to commit ourselves to full employment and mean it. "There is plenty of money to do what needs to be done, if we take the rich off welfare," I would say. I generally pointed out that Nelson Rockefeller testified before a congressional committee that he paid no individual federal income tax in 1971, and I concluded by saying, "We ought to sue him for nonsupport."

That kind of talk had not been heard much since Harry Truman had pointedly reminded the country that the Ford and Carnegie fortunes—and foundations—had been built, as he said, out of the mangled bodies and the blood of unconscionably exploited laboring people. I was, of course, talking about a return to basic principles of Americanism. But people simply had not heard this message in so long that it sounded radical to some of them at first.

To others, of course, what I said never ceased to sound radical. That had been true also during my short campaign for the 1972 nomination. One morning, back then, I was explaining at a breakfast with Washington reporters how I hoped to get press attention by holding a series of outdoor press conferences at various locations in the country to state my position on key issues. I had already held such a conference in front of the General Motors Building in New York City to say that, as president, I would move vigorously to enforce the antitrust laws against the automobile industry. The late Pete Lisagor, a first-rate reporter for the *Chicago Daily News,* asked a question in intentionally provocative form: "But Fred, isn't there a limit to how many places you can stand on your head and make outrageous statements?"

"First, I don't believe I'm making outrageous statements," I began.

"You know what I mean," Lisagor interrupted.

Before I could answer, veteran conservative columnist Roscoe Drummond, then aging considerably and apparently a little hard of hearing, caused an explosion of laughter that broke up the meeting when he leaned over to Lisagor and said in a voice which he obviously intended to be a confidential whisper but which could be heard to the corners of the room, "Well, *I* think he's making outrageous statements!"

This view was less prevalent in 1976. "When Mr. Harris began to campaign in the summer of 1974, there seemed to be several possible outcomes," Charles Mohr wrote in the *New York Times.* "One of the most likely was that, sooner or later, commentators and politicians would begin to denounce him as a radical. Another possibility was that he would make no significant impact at all and would go unheard.

"Instead, something quite different happened. Rather than 'excommunicating' Mr. Harris, many liberals in his party embraced his populist doctrines."

So did some of the other candidates. Once, on a Sunday morning, appearing on the CBS television program "Face the Nation," I said in alluding to Jimmy Carter's famous smile and his lack at that time of specific proposals for tax reform, that he was like a horse trader who would show you *his* teeth but not the horse's. By Tuesday night, Governor George Wallace was using those exact words as his own.

Jules Witcover, writing about me in the *Washington Post,* observed that "other candidates, notably Carter and Udall, often picked up his themes, in sometimes toned-down phrases, sometimes in identical ones, delivered with less aggressiveness."

Charles Mohr described this same phenomenon in a *Times* article. "Other liberals, such as Representative Morris K. Udall of Arizona and Senator Birch Bayh of Indiana, echoed many of the words and even some of the rhythms of the Harris campaign, particularly his unrelenting attacks on monopolistic power wielded by 'giant corporations,' his appeals for more equality of opportunity and his demands for social justice," he wrote. "Even more conservative candidates, such as Senator Henry M. Jackson of Washington and former Governor Jimmy Carter of Georgia, seemed to borrow elements of the Harris gospel."

This was a development we had not planned on. When I decided to seek the 1976 nomination, I knew that I would be outspent by the other candidates in New Hampshire and Massachusetts—and this proved to be true. But I thought this handicap would be balanced out by my being so distinctive on the issues. What actually happened was that many of us began to sound a great deal alike.

That was good for the country. It was a major breakthrough that all of the leading candidates came to endorse full employment and expressed support for a particular piece of legislation, the Humphrey-Hawkins bill, to bring it about. All of the leading candidates spoke out for tax reform. Most of them condemned "covert actions" by the CIA. Most of them called for breaking up the monopolistic oil companies. Most came to favor granting the president at least stand-by power to control prices in monopoly industries.

And that is what a campaign should do—focus the attention of the country on the issues and educate the candidates. Some of my good friends—writer Elizabeth Drew and Senator Walter Mondale, for example—have said that it is unnecessarily grueling and demeaning for presidential candidates to have to go through the present long, drawn-out nominating process. I do not agree. For one thing, I never found it that grueling. As I have frequently said—jokingly, but truthfully—I used to pick cotton for a living, and I find campaigning much easier. Some people get up in the morning and go to work at a steel mill. Presidential candidates get up in the morning and go to Boston or Milwaukee to make a speech. It is not all that hard.

The planned *style* of my campaign was a natural outgrowth of its basic assumptions and central issues. The original memorandum set forth the general pattern: "No limousines and drivers for the candidate. He must campaign like other people live. Buses. Public transportation. Coffees in homes. Personal contact. Staying in people's homes. No campaign jets and big staffs. These will not be gimmicks; they will be financial necessities."

When Senator Mondale announced that he would no longer be a candidate for president, he said that he could not face the prospect of having to stay in Holiday Inns for a year. I did not have to worry about that prospect, because I stayed in private homes. This practice saved money, of course, but it also made the campaign much more enjoyable, and I learned a lot. I admit that a time or two, I was reminded of what W. C. Fields said about people who hate children not being all bad—but such thoughts came to me only infrequently and fleetingly.

I carried my own bags—and later on, so did the press people who followed me, although some of them had been accustomed in other campaigns to being waited on like movie reviewers, which, in a way, they are. When Peter Lisagor first heard that we did not intend to handle lodging, baggage, and other arrangements for the press, he said, only half jokingly, I think, "Fred, we thought it was sort of quaintly attractive that you planned to carry your own bags, but we never had any idea that you wanted us to do so, too."

One of the most effective and enjoyable things we did during the whole campaign was to travel coast to coast in a camper, during July and August, 1974. We started with a huge rally in Lafayette Square, across the street from the White House, and wound up crossing the Golden Gate Bridge into San Francisco, five weeks and 5,400 miles later. Along on the trip in the comfortably large Winnebago were our daughter Laura, her cousin Alexis Gover, and two wonderful staff members, Mimi Mager, who handled press and other meeting arrangements, and Don Grissom, who was our driver, trip director, and photographer. Alexis and Laura distributed the green cards and took up the contributions at each stop. I did all the cooking, as well as all the speaking. LaDonna joined us intermittently for two or three days at a stretch, when she could spare time from her duties as president of Americans for Indian Opportunity.

We called the trip "On the Road to the White House," and this phrase, along with "Fred Harris for President," was emblazoned on the sides of our camper. I always explained that I knew we were heading *away* from the White House, but that this was because I believed that the right way to get to the White House was to first go out to the people.

Long before we had left Washington, some fifty-five well-planned picnics, rallies, coffees, and other gatherings had been scheduled along our thirteen-state route. We depended primarily on our local supporters for arrangements, but two volunteer staff women, driving a van, arrived at each point a week ahead of us, like a circus advance team, to help the local people. Two other volunteer staff people were flown in specially a couple of times, to places where extra advance help with arrangements was needed.

The camper trip was about the most effective part of the whole campaign. It helped us intensify our organizing efforts in the states we visited. It was well covered by the press, and gave me and the campaign the first real burst of national publicity. The image of

me that it projected stuck, too; months later, people thought I
was still riding around the country in a camper. Later, we rented
campers again on several occasions, for brief in-state swings just
before the voting in Iowa, Oklahoma, New Hampshire, and
Massachusetts.

We saw a good deal of pretty country on the original trip, and
we scheduled some free time along the way—on the shores of
Lake Superior in Minnesota, along the Snake River in Idaho,
in the Black Hills of South Dakota and the Grand Tetons of
Wyoming, on the coast of Oregon, and in our wonderful destina-
tion city, San Francisco.

The journey was great fun, and a good many funny things happened along the way. In the beginning, before our publicity began
to get out ahead of us, not many people had heard of me or the
trip. Later on, that changed, but during the first week, especially, I
had more than a slight identity problem. Once, for example, an
entire busload of high-school students pulled alongside of us and
shouted in unison, "Who's Fred Harris?" Luckily, no press people
were with us at the time.

But the Associated Press did somehow pick up and print a report of a similar incident, which occurred at a campground shower.
I was undressing to to into the shower as another man emerged
from it, toweling off. "I see we have a presidential candidate in
the camp," he said to me.

"Uh huh," I said, trying to hurry my undressing, not wanting
to get involved. It seemed to me to be something less than an ideal
time and place to shake hands and pass out literature.

"They say his name's Fred Harris. You ever hear of him?"

"Huh uh."

"A person would almost have to be beside himself to want to
be president these days. Don't you agree?"

"Uh huh."

"Well, I guess anybody would be better than the one we got."

"Right," I said, and escaped at last into the shower.

Great friends of ours, Eugene Crawford, a Sioux Indian, and
his wife, Evelyn, traveled across Nebraska with us, riding in the
camper during the day and staying in motels at night. They live

in Omaha, where Evelyn is a school principal. Gene is director of the National Indian Lutheran Board. Everywhere I went, I announced that I intended to make Gene, who is a most formidable-looking three-hundred-pound ex-marine, my chief of protocol.

Gene got us into one of the most memorable events of the camper trip—participation in a parade, the annual county-fair parade in Hemingford, a little town in western Nebraska. We had come to a halt at a stop sign at the intersection of our two-lane highway and the town's seven-block main street. A block to our left, the parade was just beginning, coming from a side street and turning west onto Main. Gene's instant and enthusiastic inspiration carried us all along with him. Laughing and cheering, we made a quick left turn and pulled in behind a convertible with a middle-aged woman perched up on the back seat, just ahead of the high-school band. For the only time during the trip, I moved into the driver's seat. Don, Mimi, Gene, Alexis, and Laura hopped out and ran alongside the camper, passing out literature to the people who lined the street. LaDonna from one side window, and Evelyn from the other, threw buttons to the crowd. Although we were getting a good deal of applause as we moved along, the woman ahead of us never turned around. It was only when we reached the truck-bed reviewing stand and heard her introduced over the loud-speaker that we discovered she was the Republican representative in Congress from that district. The announcer called out, "and here's Congresswoman Smith, a tenacious little gal." Women's liberation apparently had not arrived in that area yet, we thought.

"And next, next . . ." the announcer began hesitantly, as we pulled even with the stand. He consulted his parade program for guidance, but found nothing there to help him. Recovering quickly, however, he picked up the name and the idea from the side of our camper, and started again, more firmly. "And next, folks, we have a candidate for president, Fred Harris," he boomed. Ahead of us, the convertible turned left, into the fairgrounds, following the parade leader. We continued on straight ahead, slowed down a little to pick up our outrunners, took a quick glance backward to make sure that the high-school band had followed the convertible and not us, and then, making a quick turn at the next corner, sped out of town, laughing almost hysterically. We had left behind, we were sure, a harried and puzzled parade marshal, cornered somewhere and trying his best to placate a bunch of local Republicans who were shouting, "Who the hell let them in here?"

I was speaking several times each day on the trip, and, of course, everyone in the group soon knew my usual speeches by heart. At one stop, Alexis and Laura sat in the front row, where the crowd could not see their faces, and as I delivered my address, moved their lips in exact unison with mine. I found their mimicry so disconcerting that, for once, I forgot what I was going to say. I was glad that they quit, then.

Gene Crawford had to help me on another occasion, when I also forgot something. I generally ended each question-and-answer session in those days by telling the Senator Gore story, the one about the old man wheeling around to say, of a senator who had threatened him, "Blindfold the son of a bitch and point him in my direction!" The punch line makes no sense, of course, unless the audience knows that Senator Gore was blind. Once, as I launched into the Gore story for the fifth time that day, I failed to mention that fact. Gene managed to attract my attention and tried to warn me, before I got to the punch line, by putting his hand over his eyes. But I could not catch his meaning. Was it something about praying? I wondered. Did he have a headache? Finally, he whispered loudly, "You forgot to say he was blind." I recovered quickly, got that detail into the story, and finished to the usual laughter and applause.

From the first, it was envisioned that our organization and staff would consist of volunteers. "One enthusiastic volunteer, with a clear understanding of the theme, style, basic assumptions and strategy of the campaign, is worth three luke-warm, paid workers," I wrote in the original memorandum. "If the campaign starts paying people, other than a small central office, there will be no end to the paying; people won't volunteer to do the same work for nothing that other people are paid to do. People with no experience, if they understand the nature of the campaign and come to it with enthusiasm, can be taught the necessary skills—press, radio, canvassing, organization. Most of them must be able to live off the land, or their own resources, in order to do so."

That concept worked marvelously well, with one very important exception. We came to feel that we should have put a skilled organizer into each major state several months in advance of the voting there. But in those days, we had neither the skilled organizers nor the money to hire them. We had to grow our own, and doing so lost us vital time which we could never make up, causing fatal delays in organizing that we could not overcome. Local volunteers can go only so far. They need the assistance and guidance of a full-time staff. In no state were we able to provide this early enough.

The great joy of that campaign was in associating with the dedicated and effective group made up of our staff people, volunteers, and supporters, in the national office and throughout the country. The Washington staff consisted of a mixture of superb professionals, like Frank Greer, who left his post as director of the Public Interest Media Center in San Francisco to become our media co-ordinator, and extremely fast learners, like Barbara Shailor, who took a leave of absence as a senior flight attendant for United Airlines to head our delegate operation. And most of them worked without salaries. As Charles Mohr wrote in the *New York Times,* "Mr. Harris had one of the largest—and most gifted—staffs in politics, and his staff members worked for nothing or next to it."

We were all very close—literally close, for the first nine or ten months, because our national office was in my McLean, Virginia, home. In the beginning, we used only the basement, which we converted into an office, but before long, we had to expand into the living room, dining room, and den on the ground floor. Next, the two-car garage was fixed up for use by the financial and printing sections of the staff. Finally, just prior to our taking over a floor in the Ambassador Hotel in downtown Washington, we even moved two construction-office trailers into our backyard, and the bedrooms and the kitchen in our home were all that were left for family quarters. It was like living up over your store. And this early arrangement gave the members of the staff a uniquely warm feeling about each other that was never lost, even after there were more than 150 full-time people, at the national office and in the field.

Putting such a staff together and keeping it together was primarily the remarkable work of Jim Hightower, who had himself once served most creditably on the staff of Senator Ralph Yarborough of Texas. When I first told Jim and Peter Barnes that I had made a final decision to run for president in 1976, each immediately said he would take a year and a half out of his life to help. Peter became our West Coast co-ordinator. Jim took over direction of the whole national campaign and also served as treasurer.

I believe people need to laugh a little—at themselves and at the world. Laughter keeps things in perspective. I was pleased when *Time* magazine's Hugh Sidey said in a syndicated television commentary, "Harris supplied more than his share of the campaign humor, which was not exactly in oversupply."

From the first, I told audiences that while the issues were terribly solemn, there was no reason we ourselves had to be solemn. Most people had forgotten that presidential campaigns could be fun. "Can you imagine old Scoop Jackson laughing?" I asked early crowds. They could not, and most of them thought the attempt would probably break his jaw.

Jim Hightower is a laugher, and he helped all of us keep perspective. Once, early on, as we were finishing up a scheduling meeting, Jim suddenly remembered that we had set aside no dates for me to make initial organizing appearances in Illinois. "Here it is, right here in the middle of the country," he said, pointing at a map of the United States. "Can't you just see Theodore White's next making-of-the-president book? 'No doubt Fred Harris would have been elected president of the United States except for the fact that he and his crack staff forgot about Illinois until it was too late.'"

Leading off at meetings of our supporters, Jim sometimes used to point to me and tell the crowd, "Unlike the other campaigns, we've got the issues on our side, and not just another pretty face —as you can plainly see." There may be a limit to how far a person ought to go to get a laugh.

Another asset we had that no other campaign could match was LaDonna. People got two for the price of one with us—and they knew it. Both in New York and in California, separately and spontaneously, our supporters almost at once brought out "La-Donna Harris for First Lady" buttons. Nobody liked that title much, but they loved the message and were wild about the buttons. We could not print enough of them. In introducing LaDonna, I used to say that she belonged to the national board of directors of every organization anyone had ever heard of—from Common Cause to NOW. I called her a "nonprofit conglomerate." And I said, truthfully, that people in Oklahoma used to tell me, "If LaDonna can't come, why don't you come yourself."

When the campaign was in full swing, LaDonna secured a leave of absence from Americans for Indian Opportunity and began to spend a large part of her time working in the campaign. We like to travel together, and we generally did so during the campaign, sometimes splitting up for separate appearances during the day and then getting back together at night. LaDonna spoke on the issues, of course, with particular emphasis on those in which she is most interested—human rights, employment, health. I liked having her speak to a new audience just ahead of me. She is remarkably warm and personal with people, singly or in groups. Without guile or planning, just by telling about us and our lives, she helped to humanize me to audiences and make me more believable.

LaDonna liked to tell about our children, too. She would say that Byron, recently graduated from high school, was working for a film maker in New York, that Kathryn was fresh out of Stanford Law School, and that Laura had just entered high school. She would point out that I was the only member of the family who was not a Comanche Indian.

Until almost the end, I declined the protection of Secret Service agents, because I felt that their presence would inevitably diminish the openness and the personal character of the campaign. Eventually, however, security problems became too troublesome and time consuming for our own staff to handle. The agents were a good bunch, and we got along well with them. Some of them had previously been assigned to Senator Birch Bayh, before he withdrew as a presidential candidate. After looking over the broad mixture of people in our crowds—long-haired, short-haired; old, young; white, black, Chicano, Indian; blue-collar, professionals— one agent confided to Fred Droz, our highly competent director of advance, "A lot of the people in *your* crowds are the kind we were worried about keeping away from Bayh's."

The most beautiful mixture of people we ever got into one room during the campaign came together in a packed ballroom in a Jackson, Mississippi, hotel. The huge crowd included some of my black friends, some of my white liberal friends, a large contingent from the Choctaw Indian reservation in that state, and as I used to say, telling about it later, "a whole lot of my red-neck kinfolks." There was some tension among the people in that Jackson meeting at first, and I felt that I had better put them at ease. So, I told them what I had said in Madison, Wisconsin, the preceding day. "I told those people in Madison yesterday," I began, "that I was on my way to Jackson, and that I was either going to put together in one room the most beautiful mixture of people who ever got together here, or the damnedest race riot, one or the other."

The people in the meeting began to nudge each other and laugh, and then we got down to the issues. Afterward, an eighty-year-old great-aunt of mine came up to me and said, "Well, Freddie, I guess we're just going to have to be for you." And a sixty-five-year-old great-uncle took my hand and held it a long time, and tears came to his eyes when he said, "I've waited forty years to hear something like that."

We asked a great deal of our staff and volunteers and supporters—and they responded most movingly. Sometimes, though, I know we asked almost too much. One night in Iowa, for example, Uncle Ralph and Aunt Wanda Harris, for the third time in a month, drove for two hours, late at night, to pick me up after a campaign appearance and take me back to sleep at their house. As we dragged into their kitchen, tired and worn out, Uncle Ralph looked at me and said, "You know, Bud, I don't think that it's nuts trying to shoot President Ford; I think it's his kinfolks."

I wish we had been as successful at gathering money as we were at assembling our staff and volunteers. Luckily, with a volunteer staff, we did not need as much money as the other campaigners. Our first goal was to raise at least $5,000 in each of at least twenty states, so we could qualify for federal matching funds. It was a great day when we passed that tough hurdle. Thereafter, every dime we raised became two. But the going was still slow. We took up collections at every meeting. Our supporters held garage sales and bake sales. We sponsored simultaneous "Neighbors Night" fund-raising coffees throughout the country, and I spoke to the participants in a nationwide radio broadcast. We solicited contributions cold, by mail. Toward the end of the campaign, Pete Seeger and Tom Paxton and others entertained at our fund-raisers, and Arlo Guthrie and his band, Shenandoah, did twenty-seven concerts for us. Most of all, we kept going back to our list of "green card" supporters, which had grown to about fifty thousand names by the time we quit. Looking back now, I think we should probably have put more early emphasis on direct-mail appeals and on concerts. But neither of these activities made any money the first time around—and in the beginning, it was understood that the Federal Election Commission would match only the *net* amount raised. The commission finally decided to match the *gross* amount, and that saved our lives for a while.

But really, raising money is not a different function from campaigning. They are inextricable. The 1974 memorandum described the situation correctly: "A people's campaign will generate its own money; peck sacks of money won't save a bad campaign." I was not surprised when the lavishly financed efforts of Senator Lloyd Bentsen of Texas and Governor George Wallace began to fizzle.

We did *not* have a bad campaign. We had a really good one. But getting contributions became almost impossible after my disappointing showings in the first few contests for delegates. The campaign died, and so did our ability to raise the necessary money to resurrect it.

There was nothing the matter with our strategy, and we came close to making it work. Had we received a few percentage points more in the first key states, we would have been answering the question "How in the world did you do it?" instead of "What in the world went wrong?"

Our goal, as stated in the original memorandum, was to place among the top three in the first contests, such as the New Hampshire primary; to emerge in the top two in the middle contests, such as the one in Wisconsin; and to run first in the last contests, in Ohio, for example. "The candidate does not have to run *number one* in the New Hampshire primary, because the 'conventional wisdom' of the national press and political officials and observers will be that he will not even make a *showing* there," I wrote in the 1974 memorandum. I went on to say, "History indicates that the conventional political wisdom is *always* wrong—not sometimes wrong, but always wrong." Unfortunately, this time, it was wrong about Jimmy Carter, not about me.

I knew from the first that the winning candidate had to beat the "expectations." And initially I did so, running second to Bayh for the endorsement of the New Democratic Coalition in New York, and coming in first in the voting of two other liberal groups, Massachusetts Citizens for Participation in Political Action and Texas Democrats. I did it, too, by coming in a respectable third in the Iowa precinct caucuses, after which I rightly said in a press conference, "The winnowing out process has begun, and I've been winnowed in." That statement was true, but not for long.

I held on through the Oklahoma caucuses, staying alive even though I was attacking the oil companies on their home grounds, and taking on Wallace, Bentsen, and Carter in a state not known lately as a hotbed of liberalism. I ran second there to Carter, and this result was regarded as acceptable only because I was no longer a senator from Oklahoma and indeed was no longer a resident of the state.

Then, in New Hampshire, I received just 11 percent of the vote, falling to a disappointing fourth place. The handwriting was on the wall, and we all knew it that night. I tried to be as cheerful as possible under the circumstances, saying to my supporters, when the results were in, "The problem was that the 'little people' couldn't reach the levers, so, from now on, we're going to have to see to it that stools are provided in all the voting booths."

Because of my showing in New Hampshire, I was out of the news and contributions trickled to a halt; and there proved to be no stools available in the voting booths of Massachusetts, either, the following week. I could garner only 9 percent of the Massachusetts vote and run no better than fifth. Although I placed ahead of Bayh and former Peace Corp director Sargent Shriver, this showing was not good enough. Like both of them, I was really finished then, although I tried my best to keep on going.

I decided to skip the Illinois, Wisconsin, and New York primaries and make a stand somewhat later, in Pennsylvania, but long before that day came, it was clear that the ground had fallen out from under me. So I announced out.

My staff and supporters would never have forgiven me if I had quit any earlier. If I had made my announcement before it became obvious to most of them, too, that everything was over, they would have felt betrayed, felt that all their work had been thrown away. It was tough enough as it was to convince some of them that I had no choice other than withdrawal from active campaigning. Quite a few never gave up. But most had seen it coming for a long time, so there was not nearly so much sadness and recrimination at the end of our campaign as usually characterizes such losing efforts.

While the crowd of friends and supporters that gathered in the ballroom of the Ambassador Hotel in Washington on April 8, 1976, to hear my withdrawal statement was not exactly a festive one, neither was it overly hangdog in mood. There were tears, to be sure, especially when LaDonna spoke and when I finished reading my prepared statement. But there was laughter too, and by and large, those who had worked in the campaign felt good about it and about themselves. "There was considerable potential for tears as Mr. Harris stood before his followers and friends, but he did not let his full-scale campaign end that way," Charles Mohr reported in the *New York Times*. "Mr. Harris turned the occasion into an unusual—but, for him characteristic—moment of emotion, warmth and unpretentious retrospection." That is, indeed, what I tried for.

"Neither I nor my campaign have come to the attention of enough people," I said. "There are probably several reasons for this, the most important of which was lack of money, a fundamental problem made worse by the delay in reconstituting the Federal Election Commission."

I said that it was too soon for solid assessments and too late for might-have-beens, and then continued, "It is enough for now to say that you and I shared a vision of what kind of country this ought to be, that we did what we could toward making that vision a reality, that we had some effect on our country's thinking and future, and that we may yet have more before we're through."

I know we can put America back together again—across race, age, sex, and regional lines—because we began to do so in my campaign. All we have to do is, first, get people's attention and, then, give them a glimpse of what kind of country this can be: a country where a young married couple would not have to worry about how they were going to pay their baby's doctor bills, where an older person would not have to give up lunch or breakfast in order to be able to buy medicines, where everyone willing and able to work would have a useful job at decent pay, and where our foreign policy, once again, would be based on principle, so that our people would have renewed cause for pride in calling themselves Americans in the last quarter of the twentieth century.

At that final gathering in the Ambassador ballroom, a reporter asked when the decision to withdraw had been made. I answered that it had become final on the morning after the New York and Wisconsin primaries; I had spent no money or effort there but had mistakenly expected that I might nevertheless gain at least a handful of delegates. I explained that after Massachusetts, we had hoped to leapfrog the intervening contests and devote all our resources, staff, and effort to the Pennsylvania primary, but that, reluctantly, we had been forced to come to the conclusion that the campaign could not be revived. "We didn't do well enough in the early contests to call it victory," I said, "and we didn't do so poorly as to call it defeat; we ran just well enough to keep going. We didn't know what to call it, so we just decided to call it quits." Those words, paraphrasing a country-and-western song, dried up most of the tears, some of which were in the eyes of reporters.

What went wrong? Not much, really, I answered. My position on the issues did not prove to be as distinctive as I had expected, and I was therefore less able to overcome the handicap of being outspent by the leading candidates—but I said that I felt it was a plus for the country that other candidates had picked up some of my issues. I said that we had somehow not taken proper account in our campaign planning of the time and effort I would have to spend in Oklahoma between the Iowa caucuses and the New Hampshire and Massachusetts primaries. While I was tied down in Oklahoma, Udall, for example, had been able to devote all his time to those crucial New England states and bring his campaign to life again, after a poor fourth-place finish in Iowa.

Did I believe I had been fairly treated by the working press? Yes, I did. I went on to say, with respect to the campaign as a whole, that while it was indeed too early for solid assessments, two problems inherent in the present system were already evident. First, despite the effects of the recent financing reforms, success in raising money was still of enormous importance in a campaign. Second, and of even greater significance, I said, was the problem that a candidate who did not run well in the first two contests could thereafter get neither money nor media attention, while the candidate who did run first in those contests became an instant celebrity—and received *both* a new flow of contributions and saturation, free publicity. The week after the New Hampshire primary, Jimmy Carter's picture was on the covers of *Time* magazine and *Newsweek*. The morning after the New Hampshire primary—and the total vote difference between Carter and me was awfully small—I lost even those few television and newspaper reporters who up to then had been assigned to me. I made it clear at the withdrawal press conference that this turn of events had come as no surprise to me, and I said, "I don't rail against that, because I expected to use that very system."

The day before I made my withdrawal announcement, I had gone to tell George McGovern and Hubert Humphrey what I was about to do, and I had talked with Morris Udall about it by telephone. McGovern and I discussed how Udall's close, second-place finish behind Jimmy Carter in Wisconsin would have been viewed by the press as a victory, if Udall had not stated in advance that he needed to run first there. The perception *is* the reality in presidential campaigns, I said. McGovern agreed, and pointed out that in 1972, Muskie had actually beaten him in New Hampshire, with 46 percent of the vote to McGovern's 37 percent. "It was a clean victory for Ed," McGovern said, "but the press wrote it up as a victory for me and as a loss for him, because he was *expected* to get more than 50 percent of the vote."

A few minutes later, as I was leaving the New Senate Office Building, I ran into Senator Muskie. I told him about my plan to withdraw from active campaigning, and then we also talked, as we walked along, about how Udall's Wisconsin showing would have helped him, except that he had announced a higher goal than he achieved. "The perception *is* the reality in presidential campaigns," I said again, for the second time in fifteen minutes.

"I know it well," Muskie responded. "The press killed me in New Hampshire, even though I clearly won there."

"That's right," I said at once. "You got 46 percent of the vote, and McGovern got only 37 percent."

Afterward, I thought Muskie must have wondered how I had those exact figures so readily available. At the time, what occurred to me was a story Morris Udall had told on himself during the campaign. Mo said that he went into a barbershop in New Hampshire one day, and shook hands with the barber and his customer, saying, "Hi, I'm Mo Udall; I'm running for president," and the barber responded, "Yeah, we were just laughing about that yesterday." When Ed Muskie spoke about how the press had killed him in New Hampshire, though he had won, I was tempted for a fleeting second to say, "Yeah, we were just laughing about that a few minutes ago."

At the final press conference, I suggested, somewhat tentatively, that the harsh effect of the "expectations" system—and the disproportionate influence of the early primaries—might be ameliorated somewhat if the law required that free or minimum-cost television time be made available to presidential candidates who qualified for federal matching funds, no matter how they did in the first contests.

Would I throw my support to any of the other candidates? I responded that it seemed to me that there was not all that much to throw, and that I felt about that question as I had felt about taking on Secret Service protection after the Massachusetts primary. The situation, I said, reminded me of the story about the fellow down home who ran for sheriff but got barely enough votes to count. The next day he showed up on the main street with a pistol strapped to his hip. When someone said to him, "Woody, why are you carrying that gun; you didn't get elected sheriff?" he replied, "Listen, anybody who doesn't have any more friends than I do needs all the protection he can get."

I was in Madison Square Garden for the Democratic convention —to see a lot of good friends, to say thanks to those who had helped out in my campaign, and to show my public support for Jimmy Carter. I felt good about the convention. The picture was one of co-operation and coalition. Jimmy Carter, in obtaining the nomination, brought the Democratic south and the Democratic north back together, while at the same time making the strongest possible statements on civil rights, and enjoying, as a part of his bedrock foundation, the solid support of blacks. Television commentators and others called the convention dull. I called it historic.

And after Jimmy Carter had accepted the nomination, I was pleased that all those who had contested against him in the primaries now stood with him on the convention platform as supporters. There was Birch Bayh, a good man with Little League hustle, maybe a trifle light on the issues, but making up for this with friendliness and sincerity. There was Morris Udall, a man I thought was especially suited to be president, having grown tougher in his outspokenness on the issues as the primaries had progressed. I was sorry that Mo had announced earlier, in the heat of the presidential campaign, that he would under no circumstances be a candidate for the Senate opening in his home state of Arizona, and I was worried about reports that he had incurred a lot of personal debts in financing his campaign. There was Sargeant Shriver, truly a kind of Hubert Humphrey, Jr., as someone had put it—bubbly, committed, cheerful. There was Terry Sanford, a solid man whose public career should never have ended when he left the governor's chair in North Carolina. There was Milton Shapp, who didn't go anywhere at all in presidential politics, but as governor of Pennsylvania showed a lot of guts. There was Senator Henry Jackson, who basically was just as he appeared to be—a trifle stodgy but prepared in depth on all the issues. There was latecomer Senator Frank Church of Idaho, who came across on television as slightly stilted, but whose heart, and head, were in the right place. There was Governor Jerry Brown of California; he didn't say much in detail on the issues, but he seemed to be a serious person with a fresh outlook, one who would probably have to be reckoned with in the future.

And before Carter's acceptance speech, there had been the acceptance speech by the vice-presidential nominee, Senator Walter F. Mondale of Minnesota. Nothing so became Jimmy Carter as did his selection of a running mate. Fritz Mondale had been an inner-circle supporter of mine for the vice-presidential nomination in 1968, when the final choice had been between me and Senator Edmund Muskie. In 1976, I sent Jimmy Carter a telegram supporting Mondale. I said that he was clean, honest, correct in his views on the issues, and fully qualified to be president.

Jimmy Carter raised himself in my estimation—and in that of a lot of people—both by his choice of Mondale and by the careful process he followed in making that choice. Jim Hightower, who had been my campaign manager in the presidential primaries, called me after the press conference at which Carter named Mondale as his running mate and said that he thought Carter's appearance on that occasion had been superb. I agreed.

I think Carter grew during the campaign, though he was already a prepared, disciplined, determined person—and those are not bad qualities for a prospective president. He came to endorse full employment as a specific national goal. A part of his acceptance speech adopted populist rhetoric and solutions—and after the Democratic convention, he even began to speak of himself as a populist. I left New York feeling that the Carter-Mondale ticket was a good one, a strong one, and one that ought to be elected. LaDonna and I did all we could toward that end.

In Washington, at a great picnic of friends and supporters on the day LaDonna and I and our daughter Laura left for New Mexico, I looked out over a crowded flower bed of familiar faces. "We will be of good cheer," I said. "LaDonna and I are proud of our association with each of you. And as I once wrote, in a composition called 'To a Butterfly':

> Dark Future shrouds her secrets well;
> Our hopes cannot the fact of change withstand.
> So, let us love this stage—and change, itself—
> And say, what else may come,
> That this, at least, was good."

Index